The Real-Time Specification for Java™

The Real-Time Specification for Java™

The Real-Time for Java Expert Group

http://www.rtj.org

Greg Bollella

Ben Brosgol   Peter Dibble

Steve Furr   James Gosling

David Hardin   Mark Turnbull

ADDISON-WESLEY

Boston • San Francisco • New York • Toronto • Montreal
London • Munich • Paris • Madrid
Capetown • Sydney • Tokyo • Singapore • Mexico City

The publisher offers discounts on this book when ordered in quantity for special sales. For more information, please contact:

Pearson Education Corporate Sales Division
One Lake Street
Upper Saddle River, NJ 07458
(800) 382-3419
corpsales@pearsontechgroup.com

Visit Addison-Wesley on theWeb at www.awl.com/cseng/

Library of Congress Control Number: 00-132774

ISBN 0-201-70323-8
Text printed on recycled paper.

1 2 3 4 5 6 7 8 9 10-MA-04 03 02 01 00
First printing, June 2000

*To Paula and my daughter Alex, who forgave my extended absences
during critical phases of house construction — GB*

To Deb, Abz, and Dan, for making it all worthwhile — BB

*To Ken Kaplan and my family, who allowed me the
time and resources for this work — PD*

*To Linda, who has always been a true friend, cared for my home in my absences,
welcomed me at the airport and generally shown patience and consideration — SF*

*To Judy, Kelsey, and Kate, who gave me the
Love and Time to work on this book — JG*

*To Debbie, Sam, and Anna, who endured my frequent absences, and general
absentmindedness, during the writing of this book — DH*

*To my daughters Christine, Heather, and Victoria, and especially to my wife Terry,
who all put up with my strange working hours — MT*

*To the Stanford Inn-by-the-Sea, the Chicago Hilton, and the Chateau Laurier for
providing space for a bunch of geeks to hang out; and to the Beaver Tail vendors by the
Rideau Canal for providing a yummy distraction.*

Contents

Caveat

This edition of *The Real-Time Specification for Java*™ (RTSJ) is **preliminary**. It is being developed under the Java Community Process (http://java.sun.com/aboutJava/communityprocess). It will not be considered final until after the completion of the reference implementation. The experience gained from that implementation may necessitate changes to the specification. Status information on the specification may be obtained from the web site maintained by the expert group, **http://www.rtj.org**, along with updates and samples.

Throughout the RTSJ, when we use the word *code*, we mean code written in the Java programming language. When we mention the Java language in the RTSJ, that also refers to the Java programming language. The use of the term *heap* in the RTSJ will refer to the heap used by the runtime of the Java language. If we refer to other heaps, such as the heap used by the C language runtime or the operating system's heap, we will explicitly state which heap.

Throughout the RTSJ we will use the term *Thread* to refer to the class `Thread` in *The Java Language Specification* and *thread* to refer to a sequence of instructions or to an instance of the class `Thread`. The context of uses of *thread* should be sufficient to distinguish between the two meanings. We will be explicit where we think necessary.

In order to get this published and in your hands, we made some compromises in copyediting and proofreading for this first edition. It is our intention to provide this book for you to begin designing real-time applications with this specification. Please send any and all comments to: comments@rtj.org.

Authors

Greg Bollella, a Senior Architect at the IBM Corporation, is lead engineer of the Real-Time for Java Expert Group. Previously, Greg designed and implemented communications protocols for IBM. He holds a Ph.D. in computer science from the University of North Carolina at Chapel Hill. His dissertation research is in real-time scheduling theory and real-time systems implementation.

Ben Brosgol is a senior technical staff member of Ada Core Technologies, Inc. He has had a long involvement with programming language design and implementation, focusing on Ada and real-time support, and has been providing Java-related services since 1997. Ben holds a Ph.D. in applied mathematics from Harvard University and a B.A. from Amherst College.

Peter Dibble, Senior Scientist at Microware Systems Corporation, has designed, coded, and analyzed system software for real-time systems for more than ten years with particular emphasis on real-time performance issues. As part of Microware's Java team, Peter has been involved with the Java Virtual Machine since early 1997.

Steve Furr currently works for QNX Software Systems, where he is responsible for Java technologies for the QNX Neutrino Operating System. He graduated from Simon Fraser University with a B.Sc. in computer science.

James Gosling, a Fellow at Sun Microsystems, is the originator of the Java programming language. His career in programming started by developing real-time software for scientific instrumentation. He has a Ph.D. and M.Sc. in computer science from Carnegie-Mellon University and a B.Sc. in computer science from the University of Calgary.

David Hardin, Chief Technical Officer and co-founder of aJile Systems, has worked in safety-critical computer systems architecture, formal methods, and custom microprocessor design at Rockwell Collins, and was named a Rockwell Engineer of the Year for 1997. He holds a Ph.D. in electrical and computer engineering from Kansas State University.

Mark Turnbull has been an employee of Nortel Networks since 1983. Most of his experience has been in the area of proprietary language design, compiler design, and real-time systems.

Preface

Dreams

In 1997 the idea of writing real-time applications in the Java programming language seemed unrealistic. Real-time programmers talk about wanting consistent timing behavior more than absolute speed, but that doesn't mean they don't require excellent overall performance. The Java runtime is sometimes interpreted, and almost always uses a garbage collector. The early versions were not known for their blistering performance.

Nevertheless, Java platforms were already being incorporated into real-time systems. It is fairly easy to build a hybrid system that uses C for modules that have real-time requirements and other components written to the Java platform. It is also possible to implement the Java interpreter in hardware (for performance), and integrate the system without a garbage collector (for consistent performance). aJile Systems produces a Java processor with acceptable real-time characteristics.

Until the summer of 1998, efforts toward support for real-time programming on the Java platform were fragmented. Kelvin Nilsen from NewMonics and Lisa Carnahan from the National Institute for Standards and Technology (NIST) led one effort, Greg Bollella from IBM led a group of companies that had a stake in Java technology and real-time, and Sun had an internal real-time project based on the Java platform.

In the summer of 1998 the three groups merged. The real-time requirements working group included Kelvin Nilsen from NewMonics, Bill Foote and Kevin Russell from Sun, and the group of companies led by Greg Bollella. It also included a diverse selection of technical people from across the real-time industry and a few representatives with a more marketing or management orientation.

The requirements group convened periodically until early 1999. Its final output was a document, *Requirements for Real-time Extensions for the Java Platform*, detailing the requirements the group had developed, and giving some rationale for those requirements. It can be found on the web at http://www.nist.gov/rt-java.

Realization

One of the critical events during this processess occurred in late 1998, when Sun created the *Java Community Process.* Anyone who feels that the Java platform needs a new facility can formally request the enhancement. If the request, called a Java Specification Request (JSR), is accepted, a *call for experts* is posted. The *specification lead* is chosen and then he or she forms the *expert group.* The result of the effort is a specification, reference implementation, and test suite.

In late 1998, IBM asked Sun to accept a JSR, *The Real-Time Specification for Java,* based partly on the work of the Requirements Working Group. Sun accepted the request as JSR-000001. Greg Bollella was selected as the specification lead. He formed the expert group in two tiers. The primary group:

Greg Bollella	IBM
Paul Bowman	Cyberonics
Ben Brosgol	Aonix/Ada Core Technologies
Peter Dibble	Microware Systems Corporation
Steve Furr	QNX System Software Lab
James Gosling	Sun Microsystems
David Hardin	Rockwell-Collins/aJile
Mark Turnbull	Nortel Networks

would actually write the specification, and the consultant group:

Rudy Belliardi	Schneider Automation
Alden Dima	NIST
E. Douglas Jensen	MITRE
Alexander Katz	NSICom
Masahiro Kuroda	Mitsubishi Electric
C. Douglass Locke	Lockheed Martin/TimeSys
George Malek	Apogee
Jean-Christophe Mielnik	Thomson-CSF
Ragunathan Rajkumar	CMU

Mike Schuette	Motorola
Chris Yurkoski	Lucent
Simon Waddington	Wind River Systems

would serve as a pool of readily available expertise and as initial reviewers of early drafts.

The effort commenced in March 1999 with a plenary meeting of the consultant and primary groups at the Chicago Hilton and Towers. This was an educational meeting where the consultants each presented selections of general real-time wisdom, and the specific requirements of their part of the real-time world.

The basis of the specification was laid down at the first primary group meeting. It took place in one of the few civilized locations in the United States that is not accessible to digital or analog cell phone traffic, Mendocino, California. This is also, in the expert opinion of the primary group, the location of a restaurant that produces the world's most heavily cheesed pizza.

Through 1999 the primary group met slightly more than once a month, and meetings for the joint primary and consultants groups were held slightly less than once a month. We worked hard and had glorious fun. Mainly, the fun was the joy of solving a welter of problems with a team of diverse and talented software architects, but there were memorable nontechnical moments.

There was the seminal "under your butt" insight, when James told Greg that he should stop looking over his head for the sense of an argument: "This is simple, Greg. It's not over your head, it's going under your butt." That was the same Burlington, Massachusetts, meeting where a contingent of the expert group attended the 3:00 AM second showing of the newly released Star Wars Phantom Menace. The only sane reason for waking up at a time more suitable for going to sleep was that James had gone back to California to attend the movie with his wife, who had purchased tickets weeks in advance. It tickled our fancy to use the magic of time zones and early rising to see the new release before them.

The cinnamon rolls in Des Moines, which David later claimed were bigger than his head. This was an exaggeration. Each roll was slightly less than half the size of David's head.

The "dead cat" meeting in Ottawa, where Greg claimed that when he took his earache to the clinic, the doctor would probably remove a dead cat.

The "impolite phrase" meeting, also in Ottawa. The group made it into a computer industry gossip column, and our feelings on the thrill of being treated like movie stars simply cannot be expressed in this book. We are, however, impressed that a writer old enough to perceive Greg as IBM's *boy* is still writing regularly.

In September 1999, the draft specification was published for formal review by participants in the Java Community Process and informal reading by anyone who downloaded it from the group's web site (http://www.rtj.org). In December 1999, the revised and extended document was published on the web site for public review. Public review remained open until the 14th of February 2000 (yes, Valentine's Day). Then the specification was revised a final time to address the comments from the general public.

The first result of this work is the document you are reading. IBM is also producing a reference implementation and a test suite to accompany this specification.

Acknowledgments

The reader should consider this work truly a collaborative effort. Many people contributed in diverse ways. Unlike most traditional published books this work is the result of effort and contribution from engineers, executives, administrators, marketing and product managers, industry consultants, and university faculty members spread across more than two dozen companies and organizations from around the globe. It is also the result of a new and unique method for developing software, The Java Community Process.

We'll start at the beginning. Many of the technical contributors came together at a series of forums conceived and hosted by Lisa Carnahan at the National Institute for Standards and Technology. One of the authors, Greg Bollella, was instrumental, along with Lisa, in the early establishment of the organization of the future authors. He thanks his managers at IBM, Ruth Taylor, Rod Smith, and Pat Sueltz, for (in their words) being low-maintenance managers and for allowing Greg the freedom to pursue his goal.

The Java Community Process was developed at Sun Microsystems by Jim Mitchell, Ken Urquhart, and others to allow and promote the broad involvement of the computer industry in the development of the Java™ platform. We thank them and all those at Sun and other companies who reviewed the initial proposals of the process. Vicki Shipkowitz the embedded Java product manager at Sun has also helped the Real-Time for Java Expert Group with logistics concerning demonstrations and presentations of the RTSJ.

The Real-Time for Java Expert Group comprises an engineering team and a consultant team. The authors of this work are the primary engineers and we sincerely thank the consultants, mentioned by name previously, for their efforts during the early design phase and for reviewing various drafts. Along the way Ray Kamin, Wolfgang Pieb, and Edward Wentworth replaced three of the original consultants and we thank them for their effort as well.

We thank all those, but especially Kirk Reinholtz of NASA's Jet Propulsion Lab, who submitted comments during the participant and public reviews.

We thank Lisa Friendly, the Java Series editor at Sun Microsystems, and Mike Hendrickson, and Julie DiNicola at Addison-Wesley for their effort in the preparation of this book.

We all thank Russ Richards at DISA for his support of our effort.

We thank Kevin Russell and Bill Foote of Sun Microsystems who worked hard during the NIST sponsored requirements phase.

Although they have much left to do and will likely give us more work as they implement the RTSJ, we thank the reference implementation team at IBM. Peter Haggar leads the team of David Wendt and Jim Mickelson. Greg also thanks them for their efforts on the various robot demonstrations he used in his talks about the RTSJ.

Greg would like to personally thank his dissertation advisor Kevin Jeffay for his guidance.

We thank Robin Coron and Feng Liu, administrative assistants at Sun Microsystems and IBM, respectively, for their logistical support.

A Note on Format

We used `javadoc` on Java source files to produce most of this book (see the Colophon for more details) and thus many references to class, interface, and method names use the `@link` construct to produce a hyperlink in the (more typical) html formatted output. Of course, clicking on the hyperlink in the html formatted version will display the definition of the class. We tried to preserve this hyperlink characteristic in the book by including on each occurrence of a name the page number of its definition as a trailing subscript. Let us know if this is a useful feature (comments@rtj.org).

Foreword

I expect *The Real-Time Specification for Java* to become the first real-time programming language to be both commercially and technologically successful.

Other programming languages have been intended for use in the real-time computing domain. However, none has been commercially successful in the sense of being significantly adopted in that domain. Many were academic research projects. Most did not focus on the core real-time issues of managing computing resources in order to satisfy application timeliness requirements. Instead, they typically emphasized the orthogonal (albeit important) topic of concurrency and other topics important to the whole field of embedded computing systems (of which real-time computing systems are a subset).

Ada 95, including its Real-Time Systems Annex D, has probably been the most successful real-time language, in terms of both adoption and real-time technology. One reason is that Ada is unusually effective (among real-time languages and also operating systems) across the real-time computing system spectrum, from programming-in-the-small in traditional device-level control subsystems, to programming-in-the-large in enterprise command and control systems. Despite that achievement, a variety of nontechnical factors crippled Ada's commercial success.

When James Gosling introduced the Java programming language in 1995, it appeared irrelevant to the real-time computing field, based on most of its initial purposes and its design. Indeed, some of its fundamental principles were antithetical to those of real-time computing. To facilitate its major goal of operating system and hardware independence, the language was deliberately given a weak vocabulary in areas such as thread behavior, synchronization, interrupts, memory management, and input/output. However, these are among the critical areas needing explicit management (by the language or the operating system) for meeting application timeliness requirements.

Nevertheless, the Java platform's promise of "Write Once, Run Anywhere," together with the Java language's appeal as a programming language *per se*, offer far greater cost-savings potential in the real-time (and more broadly, the embedded) domain than in the desktop and server domains. Desktops are dominated by the "Wintel" duopoly; servers have only a few processor types and operating systems.

Real-time computing systems have tens of different processor types and many tens of different operating system products (not counting the custom-made ones that currently constitute about half of the installations). The POSIX standard hasn't provided the intended real-time application portability because it permits widely varying subsets to be implemented. The Java platform is already almost ubiquitous. The real-time Java platform's necessarily qualified promise of "Write Once Carefully, Run Anywhere Conditionally" is nevertheless the best prospective opportunity for application re-usability.

The overall challenge was to reconcile the intrinsically divergent natures of the Java language and most of real-time computing. Compatibility of the Real-Time Specification for Java and the Java Language Specification had to be maintained, while making the former cost-effective for real-time computing systems.

Most people involved in, and even aware of, the real-time Java effort, including the authors of this book and me, were initially very skeptical about the feasibility of adequately meeting this challenge.

The real-time Java community took two important and unusual initial steps before forming the Real-Time for Java Expert Group under Sun's Java Community Process.

The first step was to convene many representatives of the real-time community a number of times (under the auspices of the National Institute for Standards and Technology), to achieve and document consensus on the requirements for the Real-Time Specification for Java. Not surprisingly, when this consensus emerged, it included mandatory requirements for building the kind of smaller scale, static, real-time subsystems familiar to current practitioners using C and C++.

More surprisingly, the consensus also included mandatory and optional requirements for accommodating advanced dynamic and real-time resource management technologies, such as asynchronous transfer of control and timeliness-based scheduling policies, and for building larger scale real-time systems. The primary impetus for these dynamic and programming-in-the-large, real-time requirements came from the communities already using the Java language, or using the Ada language, or building defense (primarily command and control) systems.

The second, concomitant, step was to establish an agreed-upon lexicon of real-time computing concepts and terms to enable this dialog about, and consensus on, the requirements for the Real-Time Specification for Java. As unlikely as it may seem to those outside of the real-time community, real-time computing concepts and terms are normally not used in a well-defined way (except by most real-time researchers).

The next step toward the realization of the Java language's potential for the present and the future of real-time computing is defining and writing the Real-Time

Specification for Java, the first version of which is in this book. Understanding this specification will also improve the readers' understanding of both the Java language and real-time computing systems as well.

Greg Bollella was an ideal leader for this specification team. He recruited a well balanced group of real-time and Java language experts. His background in both practical and theoretical real-time computing prepared him for gently but resolutely guiding the team's rich and intense discussions into a coherent specification.

Of course, more work remains, including documenting use cases and examples; performing implementations and evaluations; gaining experience from deployed products; and iterations on *The Real-Time Specification for Java.* The Distributed Real-Time Specification for Java also lies ahead.

The real-time Java platform is prepared not just to provide cost-reduced functional parity with current mainstream real-time computing practice and products, but also to play a leadership role as real-time computing practice moves forward in the Internet age.

E. Douglas Jensen
Sherborn, MA

CHAPTER 1

Introduction

This book is a preliminary release of *The Real-Time Specification for Java™* (RTSJ). The final version will be available with the release of the reference implementation.

The Real-Time for Java Expert Group (RTJEG), convened under the Java Community Process and JSR-000001, has been given the responsibility of producing a specification for extending *The Java Language Specification* and *The Java Virtual Machine Specification* and of providing an Application Programming Interface that will enable the creation, verification, analysis, execution, and management of Java threads whose correctness conditions include timeliness constraints (also known as real-time threads). This introduction describes the guiding principles that the RTJEG created and used during our work, a description of the real-time Java requirements developed under the auspices of The National Institute for Standards and Technology (NIST), and a brief, high-level description of each of the seven areas we identified as requiring enhancements to accomplish our goal.

Guiding Principles

The guiding principles are high-level statements that delimit the scope of the work of the RTJEG and introduce compatibility requirements for *The Real-Time Specification for Java.*

Applicability to Particular Java Environments: The RTSJ shall not include specifications that restrict its use to particular Java environments, such as a particular version of the Java Development Kit, the Embedded Java Application Environment, or the Java™ 2 Platform, Micro Edition (J2ME™).

Backward Compatibility: The RTSJ shall not prevent existing, properly written, non-real-time Java programs from executing on implementations of the RTSJ.

Write Once, Run Anywhere™: The RTSJ should recognize the importance of "Write Once, Run Anywhere," but it should also recognize the difficulty of achieving WORA for real-time programs and not attempt to increase or maintain binary portability at the expense of predictability.

Current Practice vs. Advanced Features: The RTSJ should address current real-time system practice as well as allow future implementations to include advanced features.

Predictable Execution: The RTSJ shall hold predictable execution as first priority in all tradeoffs; this may sometimes be at the expense of typical general-purpose computing performance measures.

No Syntactic Extension: In order to facilitate the job of tool developers, and thus to increase the likelihood of timely implementations, the RTSJ shall not introduce new keywords or make other syntactic extensions to the Java language.

Allow Variation in Implementation Decisions: The RTJEG recognizes that implementations of the RTSJ may vary in a number of implementation decisions, such as the use of efficient or inefficient algorithms, tradeoffs between time and space efficiency, inclusion of scheduling algorithms not required in the minimum implementation, and variation in code path length for the execution of byte codes. The RTSJ should not mandate algorithms or specific time constants for such, but require that the semantics of the implementation be met. The RTSJ offers implementers the flexibility to create implementations suited to meet the requirements of their customers.

Overview of the Seven Enhanced Areas

In each of the seven sections that follow we give a brief statement of direction for each area. These directions were defined at the first meeting of the eight primary engineers in Mendocino, California, in late March 1999, and further clarified through late September 1999.

Thread Scheduling and Dispatching: In light of the significant diversity in scheduling and dispatching models and the recognition that each model has wide applicability in the diverse real-time systems industry, we concluded that our direction for a scheduling specification would be to allow an underlying scheduling mechanism to be used by real-time Java threads but that we would not specify in advance the exact nature of all (or even a number of) possible scheduling mechanisms. The specification is constructed to allow implementations to provide unanticipated scheduling algorithms. Implementations will allow the programmatic assignment of parameters appropriate for the underlying scheduling mechanism as well as providing any necessary methods for the creation, management, admittance, and termination of real-time Java threads. We also expect that, for now, particular thread scheduling and dispatching mechanisms are bound to an implementation. However, we provide enough flexibility in the thread scheduling framework to allow future versions of the specification to build on this release and allow the dynamic loading of scheduling policy modules.

To accomodate current practice the RTSJ requires a base scheduler in all implementations. The required base scheduler will be familiar to real-time system programmers. It is priority-based, preemptive, and must have at least 28 unique priorities.

Memory Management: We recognize that automatic memory management is a particularly important feature of the Java programming environment, and we sought a direction that would allow, as much as possible, the job of memory management to be implemented automatically by the underlying system and not intrude on the programming task. Additionally, we understand that many automatic memory management algorithms, also known as garbage collection (GC), exist, and many of those apply to certain classes of real-time programming styles and systems. In our attempt to accommodate a diverse set of GC algorithms, we sought to define a memory allocation and reclamation specification that would:

- be independent of any particular GC algorithm,
- allow the program to precisely characterize a implemented GC algorithm's effect on the execution time, preemption, and dispatching of real-time Java threads, and
- allow the allocation and reclamation of objects outside of any interference by any GC algorithm.

Synchronization and Resource Sharing: Logic often needs to share serializable resources. Real-time systems introduce an additional complexity: priority inversion. We have decided that the least intrusive specification for allowing real-time safe synchronization is to require that implementations of the Java keyword synchronized include one or more algorithms that prevent priority inversion among real-time Java threads that share the serialized resource. We also note that in some cases the use of the synchronized keyword implementing the required priority inversion algorithm is not sufficient to both prevent priority inverison and allow a thread to have an execution eligibility logically higher than the garbage collector. We provide a set of wait-free queue classes to be used in such situations.

Asynchronous Event Handling: Real-time sytems typically interact closely with the real-world. With respect to the execution of logic, the real-world is asynchronous. We thus felt compelled to include efficient mechanisms for programming disciplines that would accommodate this inherent asynchrony. The RTSJ generalizes the Java language's mechanism of asynchronous event handling. Required classes represent things that can happen and logic that executes when those things happen. A notable feature is that the execution of the logic is scheduled and dispatched by an implemented scheduler.

Asynchronous Transfer of Control: Sometimes the real-world changes so drastically (and asynchronously) that the current point of logic execution should be immediately and efficiently transferred to another location. The RTSJ includes a mechanism which extends Java's exception handling to allow applications to programatically change the locus of control of another Java thread. It is important to note that the RTSJ restricts this asynchronous transfer of control to logic specifically written with the assumption that its locus of control may asynchronously change.

Asynchronous Thread Termination: Again, due to the sometimes drastic and asynchronous changes in the real-world, application logic may need to arrange for a real-time Java thread to expeditiously and safely transfer its control to its outermost scope and thus end in a normal manner. Note that unlike the traditional, unsafe, and deprecated Java mechanism for stopping threads, the RTSJ's mechanism for asynchronous event handling and transfer of control is safe.

Physical Memory Access: Although not directly a real-time issue, physical memory access is desirable for many of the applications that could productively make use of an implementation of the RTSJ. We thus define a class that allows programmers byte-level access to physical memory as well as a class that allows the construction of objects in physical memory.

CHAPTER 2

Design

The RTSJ comprises eight areas of extended semantics. This chapter explains each in fair detail. Further detail, exact requirements, and rationale are given in the opening section of each relevant chapter. The eight areas are discussed in approximate order of their relevance to real-time programming. However, the semantics and mechanisms of each of the areas — scheduling, memory management, synchronization, asynchronous event handling, asynchronous transfer of control, asynchronous thread termination, physical memory access, and exceptions — are all crucial to the acceptance of the RTSJ as a viable real-time development platform.

Scheduling

One of the concerns of real-time programming is to ensure the timely or predictable execution of sequences of machine instructions. Various scheduling schemes name these sequences of instructions differently. Typically used names include threads, tasks, modules, and blocks. The RTSJ introduces the concept of a *schedulable object*. Any instance of any class implementing the interface `Schedulable` is a schedulable object and its scheduling and dispatching will be managed by the instance of `Scheduler` to which it holds a reference. The RTSJ requires three classes that are schedulable objects; `RealtimeThread`, `NoHeapRealtimeThread`, and `AsyncEventHandler`.

By *timely execution of threads,* we mean that the programmer can determine by analysis of the program, testing the program on particular implementations, or both whether particular threads will always complete execution before a given timeliness constraint. This is the essence of real-time programming: the addition of temporal constraints to the correctness conditions for computation. For example, for a program to compute the sum of two numbers it may no longer be acceptable to compute only the correct arithmetic answer but the answer must be computed before a particular time. Typically, temporal constraints are deadlines expressed in either relative or absolute time.

We use the term *scheduling* (or *scheduling algorithm*) to refer to the production of a sequence (or ordering) for the execution of a set of threads (a *schedule*). This schedule attempts to optimize a particular metric (a metric that measures how well the system is meeting the temporal constraints). A *feasibility analysis* determines if a schedule has an acceptable value for the metric. For example, in hard real-time systems the typical metric is "number of missed deadlines" and the only acceptable value for that metric is zero. So called soft real-time systems use other metrics (such as mean tardiness) and may accept various values for the metric in use.

Many systems use thread priority in an attempt to determine a schedule. Priority is typically an integer associated with a thread; these integers convey to the system the order in which the threads should execute. The generalization of the concept of priority is *execution eligibility*. We use the term *dispatching* to refer to that portion of the system which selects the thread with the highest execution eligibility from the pool of threads that are ready to run. In current real-time system practice, the assignment of priorities is typically under programmer control as opposed to under system control. The RTSJ's base scheduler also leaves the assignment of priorities under programmer control. However, the base scheduler also inherits methods from its superclass to determine feasibility. The feasibility algorithms assume that the rate-monotonic priority assignment algorithm has been used to assign priorities. The RTSJ does not require that implementations check that such a priority assignment is correct. If, of course, the assignment is incorrect the feasibility analysis will be meaningless (note however, that this is no different than the vast majority of real-time operating systems and kernels in use today).

The RTSJ requires a number of classes with names of the format `<string>Parameters` (such as `SchedulingParameters`). An instance of one of these parameter classes holds a particular resource demand characteristic for one or more schedulable objects. For example, the `PriorityParameters` subclass of `SchedulingParameters` contains the execution eligibility metric of the base scheduler, i.e., priority. At some times (thread create-time or set (reset)), later instances of parameter classes are bound to a schedulable object. The schedulable object then assumes the characteristics of the values in the parameter object. For example, if a `PriorityParameter` instance that had in its priority field the value representing the highest priority available is bound to a schedulable object, then that object will assume the characteristic that it will execute whenever it is ready in preference to all other schedulable objects (except, of course, those also with the highest priority).

The RTSJ is written so as to allow implementers the flexibility to install arbitrary scheduling algorithms and feasibility analysis algorithms in an implementation of the specification. We do this because the RTJEG understands that the real-time systems industry has widely varying requirements with respect to scheduling. Programming to the Java platform may result in code much closer toward the goal of reusing software written once but able to execute on many different computing platforms (known as Write Once, Run Anywhere) and that the above flexibility stands in opposition to that goal, *The Real-Time Specification for Java* also specifies a particular scheduling algorithm and semantic changes to the JVM that support predictable execution and must be available on all implementations of the RTSJ. The initial default and required scheduling algorithm is fixed-priority preemptive with at least 28 unique priority levels and will be represented in all implementations by the `PriorityScheduler` subclass of `Scheduler`.

Memory Management

Garbage-collected memory heaps have always been considered an obstacle to real-time programming due to the unpredictable latencies introduced by the garbage collector. The RTSJ addresses this issue by providing several extensions to the memory model, which support memory management in a manner that does not interfere with the ability of real-time code to provide deterministic behavior. This goal is accomplished by allowing the allocation of objects outside of the garbage-collected heap for both short-lived and long-lived objects.

Memory Areas

The RTSJ introduces the concept of a memory area. A memory area represents an area of memory that may be used for the allocation of objects. Some memory areas exist outside of the heap and place restrictions on what the system and garbage collector may do with objects allocated within. Objects in some memory areas are never garbage collected; however, the garbage collector must be capable of scanning these memory areas for references to any object within the heap to preserve the integrity of the heap.

There are four basic types of memory areas:
1. Scoped memory provides a mechanism for dealing with a class of objects that have a lifetime defined by syntactic scope (cf., the lifetime of objects on the heap).

2. Physical memory allows objects to be created within specific physical memory regions that have particular important characteristics, such as memory that has substantially faster access.

3. Immortal memory represents an area of memory containing objects that, once allocated, exist until the end of the application, i.e., the objects are immortal.

4. Heap memory represents an area of memory that is the heap. The RTSJ does not change the determinant of lifetime of objects on the heap. The lifetime is still determined by visibility.

Scoped Memory

The RTSJ introduces the concept of scoped memory. A memory scope is used to give bounds to the lifetime of any objects allocated within it. When a scope is entered, every use of new causes the memory to be allocated from the active memory scope. A scope may be entered explicitly, or it can be attached to a RealtimeThread which will effectively enter the scope before it executes the thread's run() method.

Every scoped memory area effectively maintains a count of the number of external references to that memory area. The reference count for a ScopedMemory area is increased by entering a new scope through the enter() method of MemoryArea, by the creation of a RealtimeThread using the particular ScopedMemory area, or by the opening of an inner scope. The reference count for a ScopedMemory area is decreased when returning from the enter() method, when the RealtimeThread using the ScopedMemory exits, or when an inner scope returns from its enter() method. When the count drops to zero, the finalize method for each object in the memory is executed to completion. The scope cannot be reused until finalization is complete and the RTSJ requires that the finalizers execute to completion before the next use (calling enter() or in a constructor) of the scoped memory area.

Scopes may be nested. When a nested scope is entered, all subsequent allocations are taken from the memory associated with the new scope. When the nested scope is exited, the previous scope is restored and subsequent allocations are again taken from that scope.

Because of the unusual lifetimes of scoped objects, it is necessary to limit the references to scoped objects, by means of a restricted set of assignment rules. A reference to a scoped object cannot be assigned to a variable from an enclosing scope, or to a field of an object in either the heap or the immortal area. A reference to a scoped object may only be assigned into the same scope or into an inner scope. The virtual machine must detect illegal assignment attempts and must throw an appropriate exception when they occur.

The flexibility provided in choice of scoped memory types allows the application to use a memory area that has characteristics that are appropriate to a particular syntactically defined region of the code.

Immortal Memory

`ImmortalMemory` is a memory resource shared among all threads in an application. Objects allocated in `ImmortalMemory` are freed only when the Java runtime environment terminates, and are never subject to garbage collection or movement.

Budgeted Allocation

The RTSJ also provides limited support for providing memory allocation budgets for threads using memory areas. Maximum memory area consumption and maximum allocation rates for individual real-time threads may be specified when the thread is created.

Synchronization

Terms

For the purposes of this section, the use of the term *priority* should be interpreted somewhat more loosely than in conventional usage. In particular, the term *highest priority thread* merely indicates the most eligible thread — the thread that the dispatcher would choose among all of the threads that are ready to run — and doesn't necessarily presume a strict priority based dispatch mechanism.

Wait Queues

Threads waiting to acquire a resource must be released in execution eligibility order. This applies to the processor as well as to synchronized blocks. If threads with the same execution eligibility are possible under the active scheduling policy, such threads are awakened in FIFO order. For example:

- Threads waiting to enter synchronized blocks are granted access to the synchronized block in execution eligibility order.
- A blocked thread that becomes ready to run is given access to the processor in execution eligibility order.
- A thread whose execution eligibility is explicitly set by itself or another thread is given access to the processor in execution eligibility order.
- A thread that performs a yield will be given access to the processor after waiting threads of the same execution eligibility.

- Threads that are preempted in favor of a thread with higher execution eligibility may be given access to the processor at any time as determined by a particular implementation. The implementation is required to provide documentation stating exactly the algorithm used for granting such access.

Priority Inversion Avoidance

Any conforming implementation must provide an implementation of the synchronized primitive with default behavior that ensures that there is no unbounded priority inversion. Furthermore, this must apply to code if it is run within the implementation as well as to real-time threads. The priority inheritance protocol must be implemented by default. The priority inheritance protocol is a well-known algorithm in the real-time scheduling literature and it has the following effect. If thread t_1 attempts to acquire a lock that is held by a lower-priority thread t_2, then t_2's priority is raised to that of t_1 as long as t_2 holds the lock (and recursively if t_2 is itself waiting to acquire a lock held by an even lower-priority thread).

The specification also provides a mechanism by which the programmer can override the default system-wide policy, or control the policy to be used for a particular monitor, provided that policy is supported by the implementation. The monitor control policy specification is extensible so that new mechanisms can be added by future implementations.

A second policy, priority ceiling emulation protocol (or highest locker protocol), is also specified for systems that support it. The highest locker protocol is also a well-known algorithm in the literature, and it has the following effect:

- With this policy, a monitor is given a *priority ceiling* when it is created, which is the highest priority of any thread that could attempt to enter the monitor.
- As soon as a thread enters synchronized code, its priority is raised to the monitor's ceiling priority, thus ensuring mutually exclusive access to the code since it will not be preempted by any thread that could possibly attempt to enter the same monitor.
- If, through programming error, a thread has a higher priority than the ceiling of the monitor it is attempting to enter, then an exception is thrown.

One needs to consider the design point given above, the two new thread types, RealtimeThread and NoHeapRealtimeThread, and regular Java threads and the possible issues that could arise when a NoHeapRealtimeThread and a regular Java thread attempt to synchronize on the same object. NoHeapRealtimeThreads have an implicit execution eligibility that must be higher than that of the garbage collector. This is fundamental to the RTSJ. However, given that regular Java threads may never have an execution eligibility higher than the garbage collector, no known priority inversion avoidance algorithm can be correctly implemented when the shared object is shared between a regular Java thread and a NoHeapRealtimeThread because the algorithm may not raise the priority of the regular Java thread higher than the garbage collector. Some mechanism other than the synchronized keyword is needed to ensure non-blocking, protected access to objects shared between regular Java threads and NoHeapRealtimeThreads.

Note that if the RTSJ requires that the execution of NoHeapRealtimeThreads must not be delayed by the execution of the garbage collector it is impossible for a NoHeapRealtimeThread to synchronize, in the classic sense, on an object accessed by regular Java threads. The RTSJ provides three wait-free queue classes to provide protected, non-blocking, shared access to objects accessed by both regular Java threads and NoHeapRealtimeThreads. These classes are provided explicitly to enable communication between the real-time execution of NoHeapRealtimeThreads and regular Java threads.

Determinism

Conforming implementations shall provide a fixed upper bound on the time required to enter a synchronized block for an unlocked monitor.

Asynchronous Event Handling

The asynchronous event facility comprises two classes: AsyncEvent and AsyncEventHandler. An AsyncEvent object represents something that can happen, like a POSIX signal, a hardware interrupt, or a computed event like an airplane entering a specified region. When one of these events occurs, which is indicated by the fire() method being called, the associated handleAsyncEvent() methods of instances of AsyncEventHandler are scheduled and thus perform the required logic.

An instance of AsyncEvent manages two things: 1) the unblocking of handlers when the event is fired, and 2) the set of handlers associated with the event. This set can be queried, have handlers added, or have handlers removed.

An instance of AsyncEventHandler can be thought of as something roughly similar to a thread. It is a Runnable object: when the event fires, the handleAsyncEvent() methods of the associated handlers are scheduled. What distinguishes an AsyncEventHandler from a simple Runnable is that an AsyncEventHandler has associated instances of ReleaseParameters, SchedulingParameters and MemoryParameters that control the actual execution of the handler once the associated AsyncEvent is fired. When an event is fired, the handlers are executed asynchronously, scheduled according to the associated ReleaseParameters and SchedulingParameters objects, in a manner that looks like the handler has just been assigned to its own thread. It is intended that the system can cope well with situations where there are large numbers of instances of AsyncEvent and AsyncEventHandler (tens of thousands). The number of fired (in process) handlers is expected to be smaller.

A specialized form of an AsyncEvent is the Timer class, which represents an event whose occurrence is driven by time. There are two forms of Timers: the OneShotTimer and the PeriodicTimer. Instances of OneShotTimer fire once, at the specified time. Periodic timers fire off at the specified time, and then periodically according to a specified interval.

Timers are driven by Clock objects. There is a special Clock object, Clock.getRealtimeClock(), that represents the real-time clock. The Clock class may be extended to represent other clocks the underlying system might make available (such as a soft clock of some granularity).

Asynchronous Transfer of Control

Many times a real-time programmer is faced with a situation where the computational cost of an algorithm is highly variable, the algorithm is iterative, and the algorithm produces successively refined results during each iteration. If the system, before commencing the computation, can determine only a time bound on how long to execute the computation (i.e., the cost of each iteration is highly variable and the minimum required latency to terminate the computation and receive the last consistent result is much less than about half of the mean iteration cost), then asynchronously transferring control from the computation to the result transmission code at the expiration of the known time bound is a convenient programming style. The RTSJ supports this and other styles of programming where such transfer is convenient with a feature termed Asynchronous Transfer of Control (ATC).

The RTSJ's approach to ATC is based on several guiding principles, outlined in the following lists.

Methodological Principles

- A thread needs to explicitly indicate its susceptibility toATC. Since legacy code or library methods might have been written assuming no ATC, by defaultATC should be turned off (more precisely, it should be deferred as long as control is in such code).
- Even if a thread allows ATC, some code sections need to be executed to completion and thus ATC is deferred in such sections. The ATC-deferred sections are synchronized methods and statements.
- Code that responds to an ATC does not return to the point in the thread where the

ATC was triggered; that is, an ATC is an unconditional transfer of control. Resumptive semantics, which returns control from the handler to the point of interruption, are not needed since they can be achieved through other mechanisms (in particular, an `AsyncEventHandler`).

Expressibility Principles

- A mechanism is needed through which an ATC can be explicitly triggered in a target thread. This triggering may be direct (from a source thread) or indirect (through an asynchronous event handler).
- It must be possible to trigger an ATC based on any asynchronous event including an external happening or an explicit event firing from another thread. In particular, it must be possible to base an ATC on a timer going off.
- Through ATC it must be possible to abort a thread but in a manner that does not carry the dangers of the `Thread` class's `stop()` and `destroy()` methods.

Semantic Principles

- If ATC is modeled by exception handling, there must be some way to ensure that an asynchronous exception is only caught by the intended handler and not, for example, by an all-purpose handler that happens to be on the propagation path.
- Nested ATCs must work properly. For example, consider two, nested ATC-based timers and assume that the outer timer has a shorter timeout than the nested, inner timer. If the outer timer times out while control is in the nested code of the inner timer, then the nested code must be aborted (as soon as it is outside an ATC-deferred section), and control must then transfer to the appropriate `catch` clause for the outer timer. An implementation that either handles the outer timeout in the nested code, or that waits for the longer (nested) timer, is incorrect.

Pragmatic Principles

- There should be straightforward idioms for common cases such as timer handlers and thread termination.
- ATC must be implemented without inducing an overhead for programs that do not use it.
- If code with a timeout completes before the timeout's deadline, the timeout needs to be automatically stopped and its resources returned to the system.

Asynchronous Thread Termination

Although not a real-time issue, many event-driven computer systems that tightly interact with external real-world noncomputer systems (e.g., humans, machines, control processes, etc.) may require significant changes in their computational behavior as a result of significant changes in the non-computer real-world system. It is convenient to program threads that abnormally terminate when the external real-time system changes in a way such that the thread is no longer useful. Consider the opposite case. A thread or set of threads would have to be coded in such a manner so that their computational behavior anticipated all of the possible transitions among possible states of the external system. It is an easier design task to code threads to computationally cooperate for only one (or a very few) possible states of the external system. When the external system makes a state transition, the changes in computation behavior might then be managed by an oracle, that terminates a set of threads useful for the old state of the external system, and invokes a new set of threads appropriate for the new state of the external system. Since the possible state transitions of the external system are encoded in only the oracle and not in each thread, the overall system design is easier.

Earlier versions of the Java language supplied mechanisms for achieving these effects: in particular the methods stop() and destroy() in class Thread. However, since stop() could leave shared objects in an inconsistent state, stop() has been deprecated. The use of destroy() can lead to deadlock (if a thread is destroyed while it is holding a lock) and although it has not yet been deprecated, its usage is discouraged. A goal of the RTSJ was to meet the requirements of asynchronous thread termination without introducing the dangers of the stop() or destroy() methods.

The RTSJ accommodates safe asynchronous thread termination through a combination of the asynchronous event handling and the asynchronous transfer of control mechanisms. If the significantly long or blocking methods of a thread are made interruptible the oracle can consist of a number of asynchronous event handlers that are bound to external happenings. When the happenings occur the handlers can invoke interrupt() on appropriate threads. Those threads will then clean up by having all of the interruptible methods transfer control to appropriate catch clauses as control enters those methods (either by invocation or by the return bytecode). This continues until the run() method of the thread returns. This idiom provides a quick (if coded to be so) but orderly clean up and termination of the thread. Note that the oracle can comprise as many or as few asynchronous event handlers as appropriate.

Physical Memory Access

The RTSJ defines classes for programmers wishing to directly access physical memory from code. RawMemoryAccess defines methods that allow the programmer to construct an object that represents a range of physical addresses and then access the physical memory with byte, short, int, long, float, and double granularity. No semantics other than the set<type>() and get<type>() methods are implied. The ScopedPhysicalMemory and ImmortalPhysicalMemory classes allow programmers to create objects that represent a range of physical memory addresses and in which Java objects can be located. The RTSJ requires a `PhysicalMemoryFactory` in each implementation. Methods on the factory object are the only way to create instances of physical memory objects. On each physical memory class `create()` methods invoke appropriate methods on the `PhysicalMemoryFactory` class to create the required instance. The factory also enforces security policies.

Raw Memory Access

An instance of `RawMemoryAccess` models a "raw storage" area as a fixed-size sequence of bytes. Factory methods allow `RawMemoryAccess` objects to be created from memory at a particular address range or using a particular type of memory. The implementation must provide a factory that interprets these requests correctly. The factory may be set by applications based on documentation from the implementation provider. A full complement of `set<type>()` and `get<type>()` methods allow the contents of the physical memory area to be accessed through offsets from the base, interpreted as byte, short, int, long or float data values, and copied to/from arrays of those types.

The byte-ordering interpretation of the data is based on the value of the `BYTE_ORDER` static variable in class `RealtimeSystem`.

The `RawMemoryAccess` class allows a real-time program to implement device drivers, memory-mapped I/O, flash memory, battery-backed RAM, and similar low-level software.

A raw memory access object cannot contain objects or references to objects. Such a capability would be unsafe (since it could be used to defeat Java's type checking) and error-prone (since it is sensitive to the specific representational choices made by the Java compiler). This capability is provided by physical memory areas, which do not provide raw access to the memory.

Physical Memory Areas

In many cases systems, needing the predictable execution of the RTSJ will also need to access various kinds of memory at particular addresses for performance or other reasons. Consider a system in which very fast static RAM was programmatically available. A design that could optimize performance might wish to place various frequently used Java objects in the fast static RAM. The `ScopedPhysicalMemory` and `ImmortalPhysicalMemory` classes allow the programmer this flexibility. The programmer would construct a physical memory object on the memory addresses occupied by the fast RAM.

In order to maintain safety, a factory object constructs all physical memory objects. The factory ensures that physical memory areas don't overlap other memory areas or raw memory access objects.

Exceptions

The RTSJ introduces several new exceptions, and some new treatment of exceptions surrounding asynchronous transfer of control and memory allocators.

The new exceptions introduced are:

- *AsynchronouslyInterruptedException:* Generated when a thread is asynchronously interrupted.
- *MemoryAccessError:* Thrown by the JVM when a thread attempts to access memory that is not in scope.
- *ThrowBoundaryError:* A throwable tried to propagate into a scope where it was not accessible.
- *MemoryScopeException:* Thrown by the wait-free queue implementation when an object is passed that is not compatible with both ends of the queue.
- *OffsetOutOfBoundsException:* Generated by the physical memory classes when the given offset is out of bounds.
- *SizeOutOfBoundsException:* Generated by the physical memory classes when the given size is out of bounds.
- *UnsupportedPhysicalMemoryException:* Generated by the physical memory classes when the requested physical memory is unsupported.
- *IllegalAssignmentError:* Thrown on an attempt to make an illegal assignment.
- *ResourceLimitError:* Thrown if an attempt is made to exceed a system resource limit, such as the maximum number of locks.

Minimum Implementations of the RTSJ

The flexibility of the RTSJ indicates that implementations may provide different semantics for scheduling, synchronization, and garbage collection. This section defines what minimum semantics for these areas and other semantics and APIs required of all implementations of the RTSJ. In general, the RTSJ does not allow any subsetting of the APIs in the javax.realtime package (except those noted as optionally required); however, some of the classes are specific to certain well-known scheduling or synchronization algorithms and may have no underlying support in a minimum implementation of the RTSJ. The RTSJ provides these classes as standard parent classes for implementations supporting such algorithms.

The minimum scheduling semantics that must be supported in all implementations of the RTSJ are fixed-priority preemptive scheduling and at least 28 unique priority levels. By fixed-priority we mean that the system does not change the priority of any RealtimeThread or NoHeapRealtimeThread except, temporarily, for priority inversion avoidance. Note, however, that application code may change such priorities. What the RTSJ precludes by this statement is scheduling algorithms that change thread priorities according to policies for optimizing throughput (such as increasing the priority of threads that have been receiving few processor cycles because of higher priority threads (aging)). The 28 unique priority levels are required to be unique to preclude implementations from using fewer priority levels of underlying systems to implement the required 28 by simplistic algorithms (such as lumping four RTSJ priorities into seven buckets for an underlying system that only supports seven priority levels). It is sufficient for systems with fewer than 28 priority levels to use more sophisticated algorithms to implement the required 28 unique levels as long as RealtimeThreads and NoHeapRealtimeThreads behave as though there were at least 28 unique levels. (e.g. if there were 28 RealtimeThreads (t_1,...,t_{28}) with priorities (p_1,...,p_{28}), respectively, where the value of p_1 was the highest priority and the value of p_2 the next highest priority, etc., then for all executions of threads t_1 through t_{28} thread t_1 would *always* execute in preference to threads t_2, ..., t_{28} and thread t_2 would *always* execute in preference to threads t_3,..., t_{28}, etc.)

The minimum synchronization semantics that must be supported in all implementations of the RTSJ are detailed in the above section on synchronization and repeated here.

All implementations of the RTSJ must provide an implementation of the synchronized primitive with default behavior that ensures that there is no unbounded priority inversion. Furthermore, this must apply to code if it is run within the implementation as well as to real-time threads. The priority inheritance protocol must be implemented by default.

All threads waiting to acquire a resource must be queued in priority order. This applies to the processor as well as to synchronized blocks. If threads with the same exact priority are possible under the active scheduling policy, threads with the same priority are queued in FIFO order. (Note that these requirements apply only to the required base scheduling policy and hence use the specific term "priority"). In particular:

- Threads waiting to enter synchronized blocks are granted access to the synchronized block in priority order.
- A blocked thread that becomes ready to run is given access to the processor in priority order.
- A thread whose execution eligibility is explicitly set by itself or another thread is given access to the processor in priority order.

- A thread that performs a `yield()` will be given access to the processor after waiting threads of the same priority.
- However, threads that are preempted in favor of a thread with higher priority may be given access to the processor at any time as determined by a particular implementation. The implementation is required to provide documentation stating exactly the algorithm used for granting such access.

The RTSJ does not require any particular garbage collection algorithm. All implementations of the RTSJ must, however, support the class `GarbageCollector` and implement all of its methods.

Optionally Required Components

The RTSJ does not, in general, support the concept of optional components of the specification. Optional components would further complicate the already difficult task of writing WORA (Write Once Run Anywhere) software components for real-time systems. However, understanding the difficulty of providing implementations of mechanisms for which there is no underlying support, the RTSJ does provide for a few exceptions. Any components that are considered optional will be listed as such in the class definitions.

The most notable optional component of the specification is the `POSIXSignalHandler`. A conformant implementation must support POSIX signals if and only if the underlying system supports them. Also, the class `RawMemoryFloatAccess` is required to be implemented if and only if the JVM itself supports floating point types.

Documentation Requirements

In order to properly engineer a real-time system, an understanding of the cost associated with any arbitrary code segment is required. This is especially important for operations that are performed by the runtime system, largely hidden from the programmer. (An example of this is the maximum expected latency before the garbage collector can be interrupted.)

The RTSJ does not require specific performance or latency numbers to be matched. Rather, to be conformant to this specification, an implementation must provide documentation regarding the expected behavior of particular mechanisms. The mechanisms requiring such documentation, and the specific data to be provided, will be detailed in the class and method definitions.

Parameter Objects

A number of constructors in this specification take objects generically named feasibility parameters (classes named <string>Parameters where <string> identifies the kind of parameter). When a reference to a Parameters object is given as a parameter to a constructor the Parameters object becomes bound to the object being created. Changes to the values in the Parameters object affect the constructed object. For example, if a reference to a SchedulingParameters object, sp, is given to the constructor of a RealtimeThread, rt, then calls to sp.setPriority() will change the priority of rt. There is no restriction on the number of constructors to which a reference to a single Parameters object may be given. If a Parameters object is given to more than one constructor, then changes to the values in the Parameters object affect *all* of the associated schedulable objects. Note that this is a one-to-many relationship, *not* a many-to-many relationship, that is, a schedulable object (e.g., an instance of RealtimeThread) must have zero or one associated instance of each Parameter object type.

    Caution: <string>Parameter objects are explicitly unsafe in multithreaded situations when they are being changed. No synchronization is done. It is assumed that users of this class who are mutating instances will be doing their own synchronization at a higher level.

Java Platform Dependencies

In some cases the classes and methods defined in this specification are dependent on the underlying Java platform.

1. The Comparable interface is available in Java™ 2 v1.2 and 1.3 and not in what was formally known as JDK's 1.0 and 1.1. Thus, we expect implementations of this specification which are based on JDK's 1.0 or 1.1 to include a Comparable interface.

2. The class RawMemoryFloatAccess is required if and only if the underlying Java Virtual Machine supports floating point data types.

CHAPTER 3

Threads

This section contains classes that:

- Provide for the creation of threads that have more precise scheduling semantics than `java.lang.Thread`.
- Allow the use of areas of memory other than the heap for the allocation of objects.
- Allow the definition of methods that can be asynchronously interrupted.
- Provide the scheduling semantics for handling asynchronous events.

The `RealtimeThread` class extends `java.lang.Thread`. The `ReleaseParameters`, `SchedulingParameters`, and `MemoryParameters` provided to the `RealtimeThread` constructor allow the temporal and processor demands of the thread to be communicated to the system.

The `NoHeapRealtimeThread` class extends `RealtimeThread`. A `NoHeapRealtimeThread` is not allowed to allocate or even reference objects from the Java heap, and can thus safely execute in preference to the garbage collector.

Semantics and Requirements

This list establishes the semantics and requirements that are applicable across the classes of this section. Semantics that apply to particular classes, constructors, methods, and fields will be found in the class description and the constructor, method, and field detail sections.

1. The default scheduling policy must manage the execution of instances of `RealtimeThread` and `NoHeapRealtimeThread`.

21

2. Any scheduling policy present in an implementation must be available to instances of `RealtimeThread` and `NoHeapRealtimeThread`.

3. The function of allocating objects in memory in areas defined by instances of `ScopedMemory` or its subclasses shall be available only to logic within instances of `RealtimeThread` and `NoHeapRealtimeThread`.

4. The invocation of methods that throw `AsynchronouslyInterruptedException` has the indicated effect only when the invocation occurs in the context of instances of `RealtimeThread` and `NoHeapRealtimeThread`.

5. Instances of the `NoHeapRealtimeThread` class have an implicit execution eligibility logically higher than the garbage collector.

6. Instances of the `RealtimeThread` class may have an execution eligibility logically lower than the garbage collector.

7. Changing values in `SchedulingParameters`, `ProcessingParameters`, `ReleaseParameters`, `ProcessingGroupParameters`, or use of `Thread.setPriority()` must not affect the correctness of any implemented priority inversion avoidance algorithm.

Rationale

The Java platform's priority-preemptive dispatching model is very similar to the dispatching model found in the majority of commercial real-time operating systems. However, the dispatching semantics were purposefully relaxed in order to allow execution on a wide variety of operating systems. Thus, it is appropriate to specify real-time threads by merely extending `java.lang.Thread`. The `RealtimeParameters` and `MemoryParameters` provided to the `RealtimeThread` constructor allow for a number of common real-time thread types, including periodic threads.

The `NoHeapRealtimeThread` class is provided in order to allow time-critical threads to execute in preference to the garbage collector. The memory access and assignment semantics of the `NoHeapRealtimeThread` are designed to guarantee that the execution of such threads does not lead to an inconsistent heap state.

3.1   RealtimeThread

Syntax: `public class RealtimeThread extends java.lang.Thread implements Schedulable`$_{35}$

Direct Known Subclasses: `NoHeapRealtimeThread`$_{26}$

All Implemented Interfaces: `java.lang.Runnable`, `Schedulable`$_{35}$

RealtimeThread extends `java.lang.Thread` and includes classes and methods to get and set parameter objects, manage the execution of those threads with a ReleaseParameters$_{43}$ type of PeriodicParameters$_{45}$, and waiting. A RealtimeThreadobject must be placed in a memory area such that thread logic may unexceptionally access instance variables and such that Java methods on `java.lang.Thread` (e.g., enumerate and join) complete normally except where such execution would cause access violations. (Implementation hint: They could be allocated in HeapMemory$_{61}$.)

3.1.1   Constructors

public **RealtimeThread**()
> Create a real-time thread. All parameter values are null. The default values for null parameter objects are dependent on the value of the default Scheduler$_{36}$ at the time the thread is created.

public **RealtimeThread**(SchedulingParameters$_{40}$ scheduling)
> Create a real-time thread with the given SchedulingParameters$_{40}$.

> *Parameters:*
>> scheduling - The SchedulingParameters$_{40}$ associated with this (and possibly other RealtimeThread).

public **RealtimeThread**(SchedulingParameters$_{40}$ scheduling,
            ReleaseParameters$_{43}$ release)
> Create a real-time thread with the given SchedulingParameters$_{40}$ and ReleaseParameters$_{43}$.

> *Parameters:*
>> scheduling - The SchedulingParameters$_{40}$ associated with this (and possibly other RealtimeThread).
>> release - The ReleaseParameters$_{43}$ associated with this (and possibly other RealtimeThread).

public **RealtimeThread**(SchedulingParameters$_{40}$ scheduling,
            ReleaseParameters$_{43}$ release,
            MemoryParameters$_{79}$ memory, MemoryArea$_{60}$ area,
            ProcessingGroupParameters$_{50}$ group,
            java.lang.Runnable logic)
> Create a real-time thread with the given characteristics and a java.lang.Runnable.

> *Parameters:*
>> scheduling - The SchedulingParameters$_{40}$ associated with this (and possibly other RealtimeThread).

release - The ReleaseParameters$_{43}$ associated with this (and
possibly other RealtimeThread).
memory - The MemoryParameters$_{79}$ associated with this (and
possibly other RealtimeThread).
area - The MemoryArea$_{60}$ associated with this.
group - The ProcessingGroupParameters$_{50}$ associated with this
(and possibly other RealtimeThread).

3.1.2   Methods

public void **addToFeasibility**()
Inform the scheduler and cooperating facilities that this thread's feasibility
parameters should be considered in feasibility analysis until further
notified.

public static RealtimeThread$_{22}$ **currentRealtimeThread**()
This will throw a ClassCastException if the current thread is not a
RealtimeThread.

public synchronized void **deschedulePeriodic**()
Stop unblocking public boolean waitForNextPeriod()$_{26}$ for a periodic
schedulable object. If this does not have a type of PeriodicParameters$_{45}$
as it ReleaseParameters$_{43}$ nothing happens.

public MemoryArea$_{60}$ **getMemoryArea**()
Get the current MemoryArea$_{60}$.

Returns: The current memory area in which allocations occur.

public MemoryParameters$_{79}$ **getMemoryParameters**()
Return a reference to the MemoryParameters$_{79}$ object.

public ProcessingGroupParameters$_{50}$ **getProcessingGroupParameters**()
Return a reference to the ProcessingGroupParameters$_{50}$ object.

public ReleaseParameters$_{43}$ **getReleaseParameters**()
Returns a reference to the ReleaseParameters$_{43}$ object.

public Scheduler$_{36}$ **getScheduler**()
Get the scheduler for this thread.

public SchedulingParameters$_{40}$ **getSchedulingParameters**()
Return a reference to the SchedulingParameters$_{40}$ object.

public synchronized void **interrupt**()
Set the state of the generic AsynchronouslyInterruptedException$_{134}$ to
pending.

Overrides: java.lang.Thread.interrupt() in class java.lang.Thread

`public void` **removeFromFeasibility**`()`
> Inform the scheduler and cooperating facilities that this thread's feasibility parameters should not be considered in feasibility analysis until further notified.

`public synchronized void` **schedulePeriodic**`()`
> Begin unblocking `public boolean waitForNextPeriod()`$_{26}$ for a periodic thread. Typically used when a periodic schedulable object is in an overrun condition. The scheduler should recompute the schedule and perform admission control. If this does not have a type of PeriodicParameters$_{45}$ as it ReleaseParameters$_{43}$ nothing happens.

`public void` **setMemoryParameters**`(`MemoryParameters$_{79}$ `parameters)`
> Set the reference to the MemoryParameters$_{79}$ object.

`public void` **setProcessingGroupParameters**`(`ProcessingGroupParameters$_{50}$
                `parameters)`
> Set the reference to the ProcessingGroupParameters$_{50}$ object.

`public void` **setReleaseParameters**`(`ReleaseParameters$_{43}$ `parameters)`
> Set the reference to the ReleaseParameters$_{43}$ object.

`public void` **setScheduler**`(`Scheduler$_{36}$ `scheduler)`
> Set the scheduler. This is a reference to the scheduler that will manage the execution of this thread.

> *Throws:* `IllegalThreadStateException` - Thrown when
>> `((Thread.isAlive() && Not Blocked) == true)`. (Where blocked means waiting in `Thread.wait()`, `Thread.join()`, or `Thread.sleep()`)

`public void` **setSchedulingParameters**`(`SchedulingParameters$_{40}$
                `scheduling)`
> Set the reference to the SchedulingParameters$_{40}$ object.

`public static void` **sleep**`(`Clock$_{110}$ `clock,` HighResolutionTime$_{97}$ `time)`
> An accurate timer with nanosecond granularity. The actual resolution available for the clock must be queried from somewhere else. The time base is the given Clock$_{110}$. The sleep time may be relative or absolute. If relative, then the calling thread is blocked for the amount of time given by the parameter. If absolute, then the calling thread is blocked until the indicated point in time. If the given absolute time is before the current time, the call to sleep returns immediately.

> *Throws:* `InterruptedException`

```
public static void sleep(HighResolutionTime₉₇ time)
```
An accurate timer with nanosecond granularity. The actual resolution available for the clock must be queried from somewhere else. The time base is the default $Clock_{110}$. The sleep time may be relative or absolute. If relative, then the calling thread is blocked for the amount of time given by the parameter. If absolute, then the calling thread is blocked until the indicated point in time. If the given absolute time is before the current time, the call to sleep returns immediately.

Throws: `InterruptedException`

```
public boolean waitForNextPeriod()
```
Used by threads that have a reference to a $ReleaseParameters_{43}$ type of $PeriodicParameters_{45}$ to block until the start of each period. Periods start at either the start time in $PeriodicParameters_{45}$ or when `this.start()` is called. This method will block until the start of the next period unless the thread is in either an overrun or deadline miss condition. If both overrun and miss handlers are null and the thread has overrun its cost or missed a deadline `public boolean waitForNextPeriod()`$_{26}$ will immediately return false once per overrun or deadline miss. It will then again block until the start of the next period (unless, of course, the thread has overrun or missed again). If either the overrun or deadline miss handlers are not null and the thread is in either an overrun or deadline miss condition `public boolean waitForNextPeriod()`$_{26}$ will block until the handler corrects the situation (possibly by calling `public synchronized void schedulePeriodic()`$_{25}$). `public boolean waitForNextPeriod()`$_{26}$ throws `IllegalThreadStateException` if this does not have a reference to a $ReleaseParameters_{43}$ type of $PeriodicParameters_{45}$.

Returns: True when the thread is not in an overrun or deadline miss condition and unblocks at the start of the next period.

Throws: `IllegalThreadStateException`

3.2   NoHeapRealtimeThread

Syntax: `public class NoHeapRealtimeThread extends RealtimeThread`$_{22}$

All Implemented Interfaces: java.lang.Runnable, `Schedulable`$_{35}$

A `NoHeapRealtimeThread` is a specialized form of `RealtimeThread`$_{22}$. Because an instance of `NoHeapRealtimeThread` may immediately preempt any implemented garbage collector logic contained in its run() is never allowed to allocate or reference any object allocated in the heap nor it is even allowed to manipulate the references to objects in the heap. For example, if a and b are objects in immortal memory, b.p is reference to an object on the heap, and a.p is type compatible with b.p, then a NoHeapRealtimeThread is *not* allowed to execute anyting like the following:

    a.p = b.p; b.p = null;

Thus, it is always safe for a NoHeapRealtimeThread to interrupt the garbage collector at any time, without waiting for the end of the garbage collection cycle or a defined preemption point. Due to these restrictions, a NoHeapRealtimeThread object must be placed in a memory area such that thread logic may unexceptionally access instance variables and such that Java methods on java.lang.Thread (e.g., enumerate and join) complete normally except where execution would cause access violations. (Implementation hint: They could be allocated in ImmortalMemory$_{62}$.) The constructors of NoHeapRealtimeThread require a reference to ScopedMemory$_{62}$ or ImmortalMemory$_{62}$. When the thread is started, all execution occurs in the scope of the given memory area. Thus, all memory allocation performed with the "new" operator is taken from this given area.

3.2.1   Constructors

public **NoHeapRealtimeThread**(SchedulingParameters$_{40}$ scheduling,
                MemoryArea$_{60}$ area)
Create a NoHeapRealtimeThread.

Parameters:
> scheduling - A SchedulingParameters$_{40}$ object that will be associated with this. A null value means this will not have an associated SchedulingParameters$_{40}$ object.
> area - A MemoryArea$_{60}$ object. Must be a ScopedMemory$_{62}$ or ImmortalMemory$_{62}$ type. A null value causes an IllegalArgumentException to be thrown.

Throws: IllegalArgumentException

public **NoHeapRealtimeThread**(SchedulingParameters$_{40}$ scheduling,
                ReleaseParameters$_{43}$ release, MemoryArea$_{60}$ area)
Create a NoHeapRealtimeThread.

Parameters:
> scheduling - A SchedulingParameters$_{40}$ object that will be associated with this. A null value means this will not have an associated SchedulingParameters$_{40}$ object.

       release - A ReleaseParameters$_{43}$ object that will be associated
          with this. A null value means this will not have an associated
          ReleaseParameters$_{43}$ object.

       area - A MemoryArea$_{60}$ object. Must be a ScopedMemory$_{62}$ or
          ImmortalMemory$_{62}$ type. A null value causes an
          IllegalArgumentException to be thrown.

Throws: IllegalArgumentException

public **NoHeapRealtimeThread**(SchedulingParameters$_{40}$ scheduling,
            ReleaseParameters$_{43}$ release,
            MemoryParameters$_{79}$ memory, MemoryArea$_{60}$ area,
            ProcessingGroupParameters$_{50}$ group,
            java.lang.Runnable logic)

Create a NoHeapRealtimeThread.

Parameters:

       scheduling - A SchedulingParameters$_{40}$ object that will be
          associated with this. A null value means this will not have an
          associated SchedulingParameters$_{40}$ object.

       release - A ReleaseParameters$_{43}$ object that will be associated
          with this. A null value means this will not have an associated
          ReleaseParameters$_{43}$ object.

       memory - A MemoryParameters$_{79}$ object that will be associated with
          this. A null value means this will not have a
          MemoryParameters$_{79}$ object.

       area - A MemoryArea$_{60}$ object. Must be a ScopedMemory$_{62}$ or
          ImmortalMemory$_{62}$ type. A null value causes an
          IllegalArgumentException to be thrown.

       group - A ProcessingGroupParameters$_{50}$ object that will be
          associated with this. A null value means this will not have an
          associated ProcessingGroupParameters$_{50}$ object.

       logic - A Runnable whose run() method will be executed for this.

Throws: IllegalArgumentException

RealtimeThread Example

The simplest way to create a thread is to accept the default parameters from the
constructor and override the run method with the desired behavior for the thread. This
can be done with a new class definition:

```
public class ReceiveThread extends RealtimeThread {
public void run() {
    //logic for receive thread
}
```

The thread can then be created with:

```
RealtimeThread rt = new ReceiveThread();
```

Thread rt will have normal priority, the value returned by
PrioritySchedule.getNormPriority(). Thread rt will have no release or memory
parameters. Before starting the thread, use the isFeasible() method on Scheduler
to determine if there is a feasible schedule.

```
if (!rt.getScheduler().isFeasible())
    throw new Exception("Whatever...");
rt.start();
```

An alternative for creating the thread would be to use an anonymous inner class based
on RealtimeThread, overriding the run method. Here is an anonymous class
implementation:

```
RealtimeThread rt2 = new RealtimeThread() {
public void run() {
    //logic for receive thread
}
```

A thread can be created with just priority information:

```
SchedulingParameters sp =
new PriorityParameters(PriorityScheduler.getNormPriority(null));
RealtimeThread t2 = new RealtimeThread(sp) {
public void run() {
    //thread logic
}
```

A real-time thread that is created with scheduling parameters but without release
parameters will have no cost information available for feasibility analysis. The
scheduler doesn't perform admission control on these nonscheduled threads. When
doing static priority analysis, it's important to use a disjoint set of priorities for the
statically analyzed (scheduled) threads from the ones assigned to nonscheduled
threads, with the scheduled threads executing in preference to nonscheduled threads.
A logical division might be at PriorityScheduler.getNormPriority(), as
employed above, although this may unduly limit the range available for scheduled
threads in systems that provide the minimum number of real-time priorities.

CHAPTER 4

Scheduling

This section contains classes that:

- Allow the definition of schedulable objects.
- Manage the assignment of execution eligibility to schedulable objects.
- Perform feasibility analysis for sets of schedulable objects.
- Control the admission of new schedulable objects.
- Manage the execution of instances of the `AsyncEventHandler` and `RealtimeThread` classes.
- Assign release characteristics to schedulable objects.
- Assign execution eligibility values to schedulable objects.
- Define temporal containers used to enforce correct temporal behavior of multiple schedulable objects.

The scheduler required by this specification is fixed-priority preemptive with 28 unique priority levels. It is represented by the class `PriorityScheduler` and is called the *base scheduler*.

  The schedulable objects required by this specification are defined by the classes `RealtimeThread`, `NoHeapRealtimeThread`, and `AsyncEventHandler`. Each of these is assigned processor resources according to their release characteristics, execution eligibility, and processing group values. Any subclass of these objects or any class implementing the `Schedulable` interface are schedulable objects and behave as these required classes.

  An instance of the `SchedulingParameters` class contains values of execution eligibility. A schedulable object is considered to have the execution eligibility in the `SchedulingParameters` object used in the constructor of the schedulable object. For implementations providing only the base scheduling policy, the previous statement holds for the specific type `PriorityParameters` (a subclass of `SchedulingParameters`). If an implementation provides additional scheduling policies or execution eligibility assignment policies which require an application visible field to contain the execution eligibility value, then `SchedulingParamters` must be subclassed and the previous statement holds for the specific subclass type. If, however, additionally provided scheduling policies or execution eligibility assignment policies do not require application visibility of execution eligibility or it appears in another parameter object (e.g., the earliest deadline first scheduling uses deadline as the execution eligibility metric and would thus be visible in `ReleaseParameters`), then `SchedulingParameters` need not be subclassed.

An instance of the `ReleaseParameters` class or its subclasses, `PeriodicParameters`, `AperiodicParameters`, and `SporadicParameters`, contains values that define a particular release discipline. A schedulable object is considered to have the release characteristics of a single associated instance of the `ReleaseParameters` class. In all cases the `Scheduler` uses these values to perform its feasibility analysis over the set of schedulable objects and admission control for the schedulable object. Additionally, for those schedulable objects whose associated instance of `ReleaseParameters` is an instance of `PeriodicParameters`, the scheduler manages the behavior of the object's `waitForNextPeriod()` method and monitors overrun and deadline-miss conditions. In the case of overrun or deadline-miss the scheduler changed the behavior of the `waitForNextPeriod()`and schedules the appropriate handler.

An instance of the `ProcessingGroupParameters` class contains values that define a temporal scope for a processing group. If a schedulable object has an associated instance of the `ProcessingGroupParameters` class, it is said to execute within the temporal scope defined by that instance. A single instance of the `ProcessingGroupParameters` class can be (and typically is) associated with many schedulable objects. The combined processor demand of all of the schedulable objects associated with an instance of the `ProcessingParameters` class must not exceed the values in that instance (i.e., the defined temporal scope). The processor demand is determined by the `Scheduler`.

Semantics and Requirements

This list establishes the semantics and requirements that are applicable across the classes of this section and the required scheduling algorithm. Semantics that apply to particular classes, constructors, methods, and fields will be found in the class description and the constructor, method, and field detail sections.

1. The base scheduler must support at least 28 unique values in the `priorityLevel`

field of an instance of `PriorityParameters`.

2. Higher values in the `priorityLevel` field of an instance of `PriorityParameters` have a higher execution eligibility.

3. In (1) unique means that if two schedulable objects have different values in the `priorityLevel` field in their respective instances of `PriorityParameters`, the schedulable object with the higher value will always execute in preference to the schedulable object with the lower value when both are ready to execute.

4. An implementation must make available some native priorities which are lower than the 28 required real-time priorities. These are to be used for regular Java threads (i.e., instances of threads which are not instances of `RealtimeThread`, `NoHeapRealtimeThread`, or `AsyncEventHandler` classes or subclasses). The ten traditional Java thread priorities may have an arbitrary mapping into the native priorities. These ten traditional Java thead priorities and the required minimum 28 unique real-time thread priorities shall be from the same space. Assignment of any of these (minimum) 38 priorities to real-time threads or traditional Java threads is legal. It is the responsibility of application logic to make rational priority assignments.

5. The dispatching mechanism must allow the preemption of the execution of schedulable objects at a point not governed by the preempted object.

6. For schedulable objects managed by the base scheduler no part of the system may change the execution eligibility for any reason other than implementation of a priority inversion algorithm. This does not preclude additional schedulers from changing the execution eligibility of schedulable objects — which they manage — according to the scheduling algorithm.

7. Threads that are preempted in favor of a higher priority thread may be placed in the appropriate queue at any position as determined by a particular implementation. The implementation is required to provide documentation stating exactly the algorithm used for such placement.

8. If an implementation provides any schedulers other than the base scheduler it shall provide documentation explicitly stating the semantics expressed by 8 through 11 in language and constructs appropriate to the provided scheduling algorithms.

9. All instances of `RelativeTime` used in instances of `ProcessingParameters`, `SchedulingParameters`, and `ReleaseParameters` are measured from the time at which the associated thread (or first such thread) is started.

10. `PriorityScheduler.getNormPriority()` shall be set to `((PriorityScheduler.getMaxPriority() - PriorityScheduler.getMinPriority())/3) + PriorityScheduler.getMinPriority()`.

11. If instances of `RealtimeThread` or `NoHeapRealtimeThread` are constructed without a reference to a SchedulingParameters object a `SchedulingParamters` object is created and assigned the values of the current thread. This does not imply that other schedulers should follow this rule. Other schedulers are free to define the default scheduling parameters in the absence of a given `SchedulingParameters` object.

12. The policy and semantics embodied in 1 through 15 above and by the descriptions of the refered to classes, methods, and their interactions must be available in all implementations of this specification.

13. This specification does not require any particular feasibility algorithm be implemented in the `Scheduler` object. Those implementations that choose to not implement a feasibility algorithm shall return success whenever the feasibility algorithm is executed.

14. Implementations that provide a scheduler with a feasibility algorithm are required to clearly document the behavior of that algorithm

The following hold for the `PriorityScheduler`:

1. A blocked thread that becomes ready to run is added to the tail of any runnable queue for that priority.

2. For a thread whose effective priority is changed as a result of explicitly setting `priorityLevel` this thread or another thread is added to the tail of the runnable queue for the new `priorityLevel`.

3. A thread that performs a `yield()` goes to the tail of the runnable queue for its `priorityLevel`.

Rationale

As specified the required semantics and requirements of this section establish a scheduling policy that is very similar to the scheduling policies found on the vast majority of real-time operating systems and kernels in commercial use today. By requirement 16, the specification accommodates existing practice, which is a stated goal of the effort.

The semantics of the classes, constructors, methods, and fields within allow for the natural extension of the scheduling policy by implementations that provide different scheduler objects.

Some research shows that, given a set of reasonable common assumptions, 32 unique priority levels are a reasonable choice for close-to-optimal scheduling efficiency when using the rate-monotonic priority assignment algorithm (256 priority levels better provide better efficiency). This specification requires at least 28 unique priority levels as a compromise noting that implementations of this specification will exist on systems with logic executing outside of the Java Virtual Machine and may need priorities above, below, or both for system activities.

4.1   Schedulable

Syntax: `public interface Schedulable extends java.lang.Runnable`

All Superinterfaces: java.lang.Runnable

All Known Implementing Classes: `AsyncEventHandler`$_{127}$, `RealtimeThread`$_{22}$

Handlers and other objects can be run by a `Scheduler`$_{36}$ if they provide a `run()` method and the methods defined below. The `Scheduler`$_{36}$ uses this information to create a suitable context to execute the `run()` method.

4.1.1   Methods

`public void` **`addToFeasibility`**`()`
Inform the `Scheduler`$_{36}$ and cooperating facilities that this thread's feasibility parameters should be considered in feasibility analysis until further notified.

`public MemoryParameters`$_{79}$ **`getMemoryParameters`**`()`
Return the `MemoryParameters`$_{79}$ of this schedulable object.

`public ReleaseParameters`$_{43}$ **`getReleaseParameters`**`()`
Return the `ReleaseParameters`$_{43}$ of this schedulable object.

`public Scheduler`$_{36}$ **`getScheduler`**`()`
Return the `Scheduler`$_{36}$ for this schedulable object.

`public SchedulingParameters`$_{40}$ **`getSchedulingParameters`**`()`
Return the `SchedulingParameters`$_{40}$ of this schedulable object.

`public void` **`removeFromFeasibility`**`()`
Inform the `Scheduler`$_{36}$ and cooperating facilities that this thread's feasibility parameters should not be considered in feasibility analysis until further notified.

`public void` **`setMemoryParameters`**`(MemoryParameters`$_{79}$ `memory)`
Set the `MemoryParameters`$_{79}$ of this schedulable object.

Parameters:

memory - The `MemoryParameters`$_{79}$ object. If null nothing happens.

public void **setReleaseParameters**(ReleaseParameters*43* release)
> Set the ReleaseParameters*43* for this schedulable object.

> *Parameters:*
>> release - The ReleaseParameters*43* object. If null nothing happens.

public void **setScheduler**(Scheduler*36* scheduler)
> Set the Scheduler*36* for this schedulable object.

> *Parameters:*
>> scheduler - The Scheduler*36* object. If null nothing happens.

public void **setSchedulingParameters**(SchedulingParameters*40* scheduling)
> Set the SchedulingParameters*40* of this scheduable object.

> *Parameters:*
>> scheduling - The SchedulingParameters*40* object. If null nothing happens.

4.2   Scheduler

Syntax: public abstract class Scheduler

Direct Known Subclasses: PriorityScheduler*38*

An instance of Scheduler manages the execution of schedulable objects and may implement a feasibility algorithm. The feasibility algorithm may determine if the known set of schedulable objects, given their particular execution ordering (or priority assignment), is a feasible schedule. Subclasses of Scheduler are used for alternative scheduling policies and should define an instance() class method to return the default instance of the subclass. The name of the subclass should be descriptive of the policy, allowing applications to deduce the policy available for the scheduler obtained via public static Scheduler36 getDefaultScheduler()*37* (e.g., EDFScheduler).

4.2.1   Constructors

public **Scheduler**()

4.2.2   Methods

protected abstract void **addToFeasibility**(Schedulable*35* schedulable)
> Inform the scheduler that this thread's ReleaseParameters*43* should be considered in feasibility analysis until further notified.

public boolean **changeIfFeasible**(Schedulable$_{35}$ schedulable,
                  ReleaseParameters$_{43}$ release,
                  MemoryParameters$_{79}$ memory)

Returns true if, after changing the Schedulable$_{35}$'s release and GC
parameters isFeasible would return true. The parameters wil be changed. If
the resulting system would not be feasible, this method returns false and no
changes are made.

Parameters:

        schedulable - The Schedulable$_{35}$ object for which to check
           admittance. If null nothing happens.

        release - The proposed ReleaseParameters$_{43}$. If null, no change
           is made.

        memory - The proposed MemoryParameters$_{79}$. If null, no change is
           made.

public static Scheduler$_{36}$ **getDefaultScheduler**()

Return a reference to the default scheduler.

public abstract java.lang.String **getPolicyName**()

Used to determine the policy of the Scheduler.

Returns: A String object which is the name of the scheduling policy used
           by this.

public abstract boolean **isFeasible**()

Returns true if and only if the system is able to satisfy the constraints
expressed in the release parameters of the existing schedulable objects.

protected abstract void **removeFromFeasibility**(Schedulable$_{35}$
                schedulable)

Inform the scheduler that this thread's ReleaseParameters$_{43}$ should not
be considered in feasibility analysis until further notified.

public static void **setDefaultScheduler**(Scheduler$_{36}$ scheduler)

Set the default scheduler. This is the scheduler given to instances of
RealtimeThread$_{22}$ when they are constructed. The default scheduler is set
to the required PriorityScheduler$_{38}$ at startup.

Parameters:

        scheduler - The Scheduler that becomes the default scheduler
           assigned to new threads. If null nothing happens.

4.3   PriorityScheduler

Syntax: `public class PriorityScheduler extends Scheduler`$_{36}$

   Class for priority-based scheduling. The default instance is the required priority scheduler which does fixed priority, preemptive scheduling.

4.3.1   Constructors

`public PriorityScheduler()`

4.3.2   Methods

`protected void addToFeasibility(Schedulable`$_{35}$ `s)`
   Inform the scheduler that this thread's `ReleaseParameters`$_{43}$ should be considered in feasibility analysis until further notified.

   Overrides: `protected abstract void addToFeasibility(Schedulable35 schedulable)`$_{36}$ in class `Scheduler`$_{36}$

`public boolean changeIfFeasible(Schedulable`$_{35}$ `schedulable,`
              `ReleaseParameters`$_{43}$ `release,`
              `MemoryParameters`$_{79}$ `memory)`

   Returns true if, after changing the `Schedulable`$_{35}$'s release and GC parameters `isFeasible` would return true. The parameters wil be changed. If the resulting system would not be feasible, this method returns false and no changes are made.

   Overrides: `public boolean changeIfFeasible(Schedulable35 schedulable, ReleaseParameters43 release, MemoryParameters79 memory)`$_{37}$ in class `Scheduler`$_{36}$

   Parameters:
          `schedulable` - The `Schedulable`$_{35}$ object for which to check admittance. If null nothing happens.
          `release` - The proposed `ReleaseParameters`$_{43}$. If null, no change is made.
          `memory` - The proposed `MemoryParameters`$_{79}$. If null, no change is made.

public void **fireSchedulable**(Schedulable$_{35}$ schedulable)
Triggers the execution of a Schedulable$_{35}$ object (like an AsyncEventHandler$_{127}$).

Parameters:

schedulable - The Schedulable$_{35}$ object to make active.

public int **getMaxPriority**()
Returns the maximum priority available for a thread managed by this scheduler.

public static int **getMaxPriority**(java.lang.Thread thread)
If the given thread is scheduled by the required PriorityScheduler the maximum priority of the PriorityScheduler is returned otherwise Thread.MAX_PRIORITY is returned.

Parameters:

thread - An instance of Thread. If null the maximum priority of the required PriorityScheduler is returned.

public int **getMinPriority**()
Returns the minimum priority available for a thread managed by this scheduler.

public static int **getMinPriority**(java.lang.Thread thread)
If the given thread is scheduled by the required PriorityScheduler the minimum priority of the PriorityScheduler is returned otherwise Thread.MIN_PRIORITY is returned.

Parameters:

thread - An instance of Thread. If null the minimum priority of the required PriorityScheduler is returned.

public int **getNormPriority**()
Returns the normal priority available for a thread managed by this scheduler.

public static int **getNormPriority**(java.lang.Thread thread)
If the given thread is scheduled by the required PriorityScheduler the normal priority of the PriorityScheduler is returned otherwise Thread.NORM_PRIORITY is returned.

Parameters:

thread - An instance of Thread. If null the normal priority of the required PriorityScheduler is returned.

```
public java.lang.String getPolicyName()
```
Used to determine the policy of the Scheduler.

> *Overrides:* `public abstract java.lang.String getPolicyName()`$_{37}$ in class `Scheduler`$_{36}$

> *Returns:* A String object which is the name of the scheduling policy used by this.

```
public static PriorityScheduler38 instance()
```
Return a pointer to an instance of `PriorityScheduler`.

```
public boolean isFeasible()
```
Returns true if the system is able to satisfy the constraints expressed in the release parameters of the existing schedulable objects.

> *Overrides:* `public abstract boolean isFeasible()`$_{37}$ in class `Scheduler`$_{36}$

```
protected void removeFromFeasibility(Schedulable35 s)
```
Inform the scheduler that this thread's `ReleaseParameters`$_{43}$ should not be considered in feasibility analysis until further notified.

> *Overrides:* `protected abstract void removeFromFeasibility(Schedulable35 schedulable)`$_{37}$ in class `Scheduler`$_{36}$

4.4   SchedulingParameters

Syntax: `public abstract class SchedulingParameters`

Direct Known Subclasses: `PriorityParameters`$_{41}$

Subclasses of `SchedulingParameters` (`PriorityParameters`$_{41}$, `ImportanceParameters`$_{42}$, and any others defined for particular schedulers) provide the parameters to be used by the `Scheduler`$_{36}$. Changes to the values in a parameters object affects the scheduling behaviour of all the `Schedulable`$_{35}$ objects to which it is bound.

Caution: Subclasses of this class are explicitly unsafe in multithreaded situations when they are being changed. No synchronization is done. It is assumed that users of this class who are mutating instances will be doing their own synchronization at a higher level.

4.4.1   Constructors

public **SchedulingParameters**()

4.5   PriorityParameters

Syntax: public class PriorityParameters extends SchedulingParameters$_{40}$

Direct Known Subclasses: ImportanceParameters$_{42}$

Instances of this class should be assigned to threads that are managed by schedulers which use a single integer to determine execution order. The base scheduler required by this specification and represented by the class PriorityScheduler$_{38}$ is such a scheduler.

4.5.1   Constructors

public **PriorityParameters**(int priority)
Create an instance of SchedulingParameters$_{40}$ with the given priority.

Parameters:
priority - The priority assigned to a thread. This value is used in place of the value returned by java.lang.Thread.setPriority(int) .

4.5.2   Methods

public int **getPriority**()
Get the priority.

public void **setPriority**(int priority)
Set the priority.

Parameters:
priority - The new value of priority.

Throws: IllegalArgumentException - Thrown if the given priority value is less than the minimum priority of the scheduler of any of the associated threads or greater then the maximum priority of the scheduler of any of the associated threads.

public java.lang.String **toString**()

Overrides: java.lang.Object.toString() in class java.lang.Object

4.6   ImportanceParameters

Syntax: `public class ImportanceParameters extends PriorityParameters`$_{41}$

Importance is an additional scheduling metric that may be used by some priority-based scheduling algorithms during overload conditions to differentiate execution order among threads of the same priority.

In some real-time systems an external physical process determines the period of many threads. If rate-monotonic priority assignment is used to assign priorities many of the threads in the system may have the same priority because their periods are the same. However, it is conceivable that some threads may be more important than others and in an overload situation importance can help the scheduler decide which threads to execute first. The base scheduling algorithm represented by `PriorityScheduler`$_{38}$ is not required to use importance. However, the RTSJ strongly suggests to implementers that a fairly simple subclass of `PriorityScheduler`$_{38}$ that uses importance can offer value to some real-time applications.

4.6.1   Constructors

public **ImportanceParameters**(int priority, int importance)
> Create an instance of ImportanceParameters.

> *Parameters:*
>> priority - The priority assigned to a thread. This value is used in place of java.lang.Thread.priority.
>> importance - The importance value assigned to a thread.

4.6.2   Methods

public int **getImportance**()
> Get the importance value.

public void **setImportance**(int importance)
> Set the importance.

public java.lang.String **toString**()

> *Overrides:* `public java.lang.String toString()`$_{41}$ in class `PriorityParameters`$_{41}$

4.7   ReleaseParameters

Syntax: `public abstract class ReleaseParameters`

Direct Known Subclasses: `AperiodicParameters`[47], `PeriodicParameters`[45]

The abstract top-level class for release characteristics of threads. When a reference to a `ReleaseParameters` object is given as a parameter to a constructor, the `ReleaseParameters` object becomes bound to the object being created. Changes to the values in the `ReleaseParameters` object affect the constructed object. If given to more than one constructor, then changes to the values in the `ReleaseParameters` object affect *all* of the associated objects. Note that this is a one-to-many relationship and *not* a many-to-many.

Caution: This class is explicitly unsafe in multithreaded situations when it is being changed. No synchronization is done. It is assumed that users of this class who are mutating instances will be doing their own synchronization at a higher level.

Caution: The `cost` parameter time should be considered to be measured against the target platform.

4.7.1   Constructors

```
protected ReleaseParameters(RelativeTime102 cost,
                 RelativeTime102 deadline,
                 AsyncEventHandler127 overrunHandler,
                 AsyncEventHandler127 missHandler)
```

Subclasses use this constructor to create a `ReleaseParameters` type object.

Parameters:

cost - Processing time units per interval. On implementations which can measure the amount of time a schedulable object is executed, this value is the maximum amount of time a schedulable object receives per interval. On implementations which cannot measure execution time, this value is used as a hint to the feasibility algorithm. On such systems it is not possible to determine when any particular object exceeds cost. Equivalent to `RelativeTime(0,0)` if null.

deadline - The latest permissible completion time measured from the release time of the associated invocation of the schedulable object. Changing the deadline might not take effect after the expiration of the current deadline. More detail provided in the subclasses.

overrunHandler - This handler is invoked if an invocation of the
schedulable object exceeds cost. Not required for minimum
implementation. If null, nothing happens on the overrun
condition, and waitForNextPeriod returns false immediately and
updates the start time for the next period.

missHandler - This handler is invoked if the run() method of the
schedulable object is still executing after the deadline has
passed. Although minimum implementations do not consider
deadlines in feasibility calculations, they must recognize
variable deadlines and invoke the miss handler as appropriate. If
null, nothing happens on the miss deadline condition.

4.7.2   Methods

public RelativeTime$_{102}$ **getCost**()
Get the cost value.

public AsyncEventHandler$_{127}$ **getCostOverrunHandler**()
Get the cost overrun handler.

public RelativeTime$_{102}$ **getDeadline**()
Get the deadline.

public AsyncEventHandler$_{127}$ **getDeadlineMissHandler**()
Get the deadline miss handler.

public void **setCost**(RelativeTime$_{102}$ cost)
Set the cost value.

Parameters:

cost - Processing time units per period or per minimum interarrival
interval. On implementations which can measure the amount of
time a schedulable object is executed, this value is the maximum
amount of time a schedulable object receives per period or per
minimum interarrival interval. On implementations which
cannot measure execution time, this value is used as a hint to the
feasibility algorithm. On such systems it is not possible to
determine when any particular object exceeds or will exceed
cost time units in a period or interval. Equivalent to
RelativeTime(0,0) if null.

public void **setCostOverrunHandler**(AsyncEventHandler$_{127}$ handler)
>   Set the cost overrun handler.

>   *Parameters:*
>>   handler - This handler is invoked if an invocation of the
>>   schedulable object exceeds cost. Not required for minimum
>>   implementation. See comments in setCost().

public void **setDeadline**(RelativeTime$_{102}$ deadline)

>   Set the deadline value.

>   *Parameters:*
>>   deadline - The latest permissible completion time measured from
>>   the release time of the associated invocation of the schedulable
>>   object. For a minimum implementation for purposes of
>>   feasibility analysis, the deadline is equal to the period or
>>   minimum interarrival interval. Other implementations may use
>>   this parameter to compute execution eligibility.

public void **setDeadlineMissHandler**(AsyncEventHandler$_{127}$ handler)
>   Set the deadline miss handler.

>   *Parameters:*
>>   handler - This handler is invoked if the run() method of the
>>   schedulable object is still executing after the deadline has
>>   passed. Although minimum implementations do not consider
>>   deadlines in feasibility calculations, they must recognize
>>   variable deadlines and invoke the miss handler as appropriate.

4.8   PeriodicParameters

Syntax: public class PeriodicParameters extends ReleaseParameters$_{43}$

This release parameter indicates that the public boolean
waitForNextPeriod()$_{26}$ method on the associated Schedulable$_{35}$ object will be
unblocked at the start of each period. When a reference to a PeriodicParameters
object is given as a parameter to a constructor the PeriodicParameters object
becomes bound to the object being created. Changes to the values in the
PeriodicParameters object affect the constructed object. If given to more than one
constructor then changes to the values in the PeriodicParameters object affect *all* of
the associated objects. Note that this is a one-to-many relationship and *not* a many-to-
many.

Caution: This class is explicitly unsafe in multithreaded situations when it is being changed. No synchronization is done. It is assumed that users of this class who are mutating instances will be doing their own synchronization at a higher level.

4.8.1   Constructors

public **PeriodicParameters**(HighResolutionTime$_{97}$ start,
                    RelativeTime$_{102}$ period, RelativeTime$_{102}$ cost,
                    RelativeTime$_{102}$ deadline,
                    AsyncEventHandler$_{127}$ overrunHandler,
                    AsyncEventHandler$_{127}$ missHandler)
Create a PeriodicParameters object.

Parameters:
> start - Time at which the first period begins. If a RelativeTime$_{102}$, this time is relative to the first time the schedulable object becomes schedulable *(schedulable time)* (e.g., when start() is called on a thread). If an AbsoluteTime$_{99}$ and it is before the schedulable time, start is equivalent to the schedulable time.
> period - The period is the interval between successive unblocks of public boolean waitForNextPeriod()$_{26}$. Must be greater than zero when entering feasibility analysis.
> cost - Processing time per period. On implementations which can measure the amount of time a schedulable object is executed, this value is the maximum amount of time a schedulable object receives per period. On implementations which cannot measure execution time, this value is used as a hint to the feasibility algorithm. On such systems it is not possible to determine when any particular object exceeds or will exceed cost time units in a period. Equivalent to RelativeTime(0,0) if null.
> deadline - The latest permissible completion time measured from the release time of the associated invocation of the schedulable object. For a minimum implementation for purposes of feasibility analysis, the deadline is equal to the period. Other implementations may use this parameter to compute execution eligibility. If null, deadline will equal the period.
> overrunHandler - This handler is invoked if an invocation of the schedulable object exceeds cost in the given period. Not required for minimum implementation. If null, nothing happens on the overrun condition.

missHandler - This handler is invoked if the run() method of the schedulable object is still executing after the deadline has passed. Although minimum implementations do not consider deadlines in feasibility calculations, they must recognize variable deadlines and invoke the miss handler as appropriate. If null, nothing happens on the miss deadline condition.

4.8.2 Methods

public RelativeTime$_{102}$ **getPeriod**()
  Get the period.

public HighResolutionTime$_{97}$ **getStart**()
  Get the start time.

public void **setPeriod**(RelativeTime$_{102}$ period)
  Set the period.

  Parameters:
      period - The period is the interval between successive unblocks of public boolean waitForNextPeriod()$_{26}$. Also used in the feasibility analysis and admission control algorithms.

public void **setStart**(HighResolutionTime$_{97}$ start)
  Set the start time.

  Parameters:
      start - Time at which the first period begins.

4.9   AperiodicParameters

Syntax: public class AperiodicParameters extends ReleaseParameters$_{43}$

Direct Known Subclasses: SporadicParameters$_{49}$

This release parameter object characterizes a schedulable object that may become active at any time. When a reference to a AperiodicParameters$_{47}$ object is given as a parameter to a constructor the AperiodicParameters$_{47}$ object becomes bound to the object being created. Changes to the values in the AperiodicParameters$_{47}$ object affect the constructed object. If given to more than one constructor then changes to the values in the AperiodicParameters$_{47}$ object affect *all* of the associated objects. Note that this is a one-to-many relationship and *not* a many-to-many.

Caution: This class is explicitly unsafe in multithreaded situations when it is being changed. No synchronization is done. It is assumed that users of this class who are mutating instances will be doing their own synchronization at a higher level.

4.9.1   Constructors

```
public AperiodicParameters(RelativeTime₁₀₂ cost,
                RelativeTime₁₀₂ deadline,
                AsyncEventHandler₁₂₇ overrunHandler,
                AsyncEventHandler₁₂₇ missHandler)
```

Create an AperiodicParameters$_{47}$ object.

Parameters:

cost - Processing time per invocation. On implementations which can measure the amount of time a schedulable object is executed, this value is the maximum amount of time a schedulable object receives. On implementations which cannot measure execution time, this value is used as a hint to the feasibility algorithm. On such systems it is not possible to determine when any particular object exceeds cost. Equivalent to RelativeTime(0,0) if null.

deadline - The latest permissible completion time measured from the release time of the associated invocation of the schedulable object. Not used in feasibility analysis for minimum implementation. If null, the deadline will be RelativeTime(Long.MAX_VALUE,999999).

overrunHandler - This handler is invoked if an invocation of the schedulable object exceeds cost. Not required for minimum implementation. If null, nothing happens on the overrun condition.

missHandler - This handler is invoked if the run() method of the schedulable object is still executing after the deadline has passed. Although minimum implementations do not consider deadlines in feasibility calculations, they must recognize variable deadlines and invoke the miss handler as appropriate. If null, nothing happens on the miss deadline condition.

4.10   SporadicParameters

Syntax: `public class SporadicParameters extends AperiodicParameters`[47]

A notice to the scheduler that the associated schedulable object's run method will be released aperiodically but with a minimum time between releases. When a reference to a `SporadicParameters` object is given as a parameter to a constructor, the `SporadicParameters` object becomes bound to the object being created. Changes to the values in the `SporadicParameters` object affect the constructed object. If given to more than one constructor, then changes to the values in the `SporadicParameters` object affect *all* of the associated objects. Note that this is a one-to-many relationship and *not* a many-to-many.

Caution: This class is explicitly unsafe in multithreaded situations when it is being changed. No synchronization is done. It is assumed that users of this class who are mutating instances will be doing their own synchronization at a higher level.

4.10.1   Constructors

```
public SporadicParameters(RelativeTime102 minInterarrival,
             RelativeTime102 cost, RelativeTime102 deadline,
             AsyncEventHandler127 overrunHandler,
             AsyncEventHandler127 missHandler)
```
Create a `SporadicParameters` object.

Parameters:

   `minInterarrival` - The release times of the schedulable object will occur no closer than this interval. Must be greater than zero when entering feasibility analysis.

   `cost` - Processing time per minimum interarrival interval. On implementations which can measure the amount of time a schedulable object is executed, this value is the maximum amount of time a schedulable object receives per interval. On implementations which cannot measure execution time, this value is used as a hint to the feasibility algorithm. On such systems it is not possible to determine when any particular object exceeds cost. Equivalent to `RelativeTime(0,0)` if null.

   `deadline` - The latest permissible completion time measured from the release time of the associated invocation of the schedulable object. For a minimum implementation for purposes of feasibility analysis, the deadline is equal to the minimum interarrival interval. Other implementations may use this

parameter to compute execution eligibility. If null, deadline will
equal the minimum interarrival time.

overrunHandler - This handler is invoked if an invocation of the
schedulable object exceeds cost. Not required for minimum
implementation. If null, nothing happens on the overrun
condition.

missHandler - This handler is invoked if the run() method of the
schedulable object is still executing after the deadline has
passed. Although minimum implementations do not consider
deadlines in feasibility calculations, they must recognize
variable deadlines and invoke the miss handler as appropriate. If
null, nothing happens on the miss deadline condition.

4.10.2 Methods

public RelativeTime$_{102}$ **getMinimumInterarrival**()
Get the minimum interarrival time.

public void **setMinimumInterarrival**(RelativeTime$_{102}$ minimum)
Set the minimum interarrival time.

Parameters:

minimum - The release times of the schedulable object will occur no
closer than this interval. Must be greater than zero when
entering feasibility analysis.

4.11   ProcessingGroupParameters

Syntax: public class ProcessingGroupParameters

This is associated with one or more schedulable objects for which the system
guarantees that the associated objects will not be given more time per period than
indicated by cost. For all threads with a reference to an instance of
ProcessingGroupParameters p and a reference to an instance of
AperiodicParameters$_{47}$ no more than p.cost will be allocated to the execution of
these threads in each interval of time given by p.period after the time indicated by
p.start. When a reference to a ProcessingGroupParameters object is given as a
parameter to a constructor the ProcessingGroupParameters object becomes bound
to the object being created. Changes to the values in the
ProcessingGroupParameters object affect the constructed object. If given to more
than one constructor, then changes to the values in the ProcessingGroupParameters

object affect *all* of the associated objects. Note that this is a one-to-many relationship and *not* a many-to-many.

Caution: This class is explicitly unsafe in multithreaded situations when it is being changed. No synchronization is done. It is assumed that users of this class who are mutating instances will be doing their own synchronization at a higher level.

Caution: The cost parameter time should be considered to be measured against the target platform.

4.11.1 Constructors

public **ProcessingGroupParameters**(HighResolutionTime$_{97}$ start, RelativeTime$_{102}$ period, RelativeTime$_{102}$ cost, RelativeTime$_{102}$ deadline, AsyncEventHandler$_{127}$ overrunHandler, AsyncEventHandler$_{127}$ missHandler)

Create a ProcessingGroupParameters object.

Parameters:

start - Time at which the first period begins.

period - The period is the interval between successive unblocks of waitForNextPeriod().

cost - Processing time per period.

deadline - The latest permissible completion time measured from the start of the current period. Changing the deadline might not take effect after the expiration of the current deadline.

overrunHandler - This handler is invoked if the run() method of the schedulable object of the previous period is still executing at the start of the current period.

missHandler - This handler is invoked if the run() method of the schedulable object is still executing after the deadline has passed.

4.11.2 Methods

public RelativeTime$_{102}$ **getCost**()

Get the cost value.

public AsyncEventHandler$_{127}$ **getCostOverrunHandler**()

Get the cost overrun handler.

Returns: An AsyncEventHandler$_{127}$ object that is cost overrun handler of this.

public RelativeTime$_{102}$ **getDeadline**()
> Get the deadline value.

> *Returns:* A RelativeTime$_{102}$ object that represents the deadline of this.

public AsyncEventHandler$_{127}$ **getDeadlineMissHandler**()
> Get the deadline missed handler.

> *Returns:* An AsyncEventHandler$_{127}$ object that is deadline miss handler
>> of this.

public RelativeTime$_{102}$ **getPeriod**()
> Get the period.

> *Returns:* A RelativeTime$_{102}$ object that represents the period of time of
>> this.

public HighResolutionTime$_{97}$ **getStart**()
> Get the start time.

> *Returns:* A HighResolutionTime$_{97}$ object that represents the start time of
>> this.

public void **setCost**(RelativeTime$_{102}$ cost)
> Set the cost value.

> *Parameters:*
>> cost - The schedulable objects with a reference to this receive
>>> cumulatively no more than cost time per period on
>>> implementations that can collect execution time per thread.

public void **setCostOverrunHandler**(AsyncEventHandler$_{127}$ handler)
> Set the cost overrun handler.

> *Parameters:*
>> handler - This handler is invoked if the run() method of the
>>> schedulable object of the previous period is still executing at the
>>> start of the current period.

public void **setDeadline**(RelativeTime$_{102}$ deadline)
> Set the deadline value.

> *Parameters:*
>> deadline - The latest permissible completion time measured from
>>> the start of the current period. Not used in a minimum
>>> implementation. Other implmentations may use this parameter
>>> to compute execution eligibility. The default value is the same as
>>> period.

public void **setDeadlineMissHandler**(AsyncEventHandler$_{127}$ handler)
 Set the deadline miss handler.

 Parameters:
  handler - This handler is invoked if the run() method of the
   schedulable object is still executing after the deadline has
   passed.

public void **setPeriod**(RelativeTime$_{102}$ period)
 Set the period.

 Parameters:
  period - Interval used to enforce allocation of processing resources
   to the associated schedulable objects. Also used in the feasibility
   analysis and admission control algorithms.

public void **setStart**(HighResolutionTime$_{97}$ start)
 Set the start time.

 Parameters:
  start - Time at which the first period begins.

Scheduler Example

An implementation may provide a scheduler other than the required minimum
scheduler. If you wish to use that scheduler to manage your threads, you need to find
out about the alternative scheduler. In some cases, the alternative scheduler may be
installed as the default scheduler for the implementation. In others, it may be
necessary to locate the scheduler in order to use it to schedule threads. The following
method shows how a scheduler implementing a policy can be located and the instance
to the singleton object obtained:

```
public static Scheduler findScheduler(String policy) {
  String className = System.getProperty("javax.realtime.scheduler.
" +
 policy);
  Class clazz;
  try {
    if (className != null
  && (clazz = Class.forName(className)) != null) {
    return (Scheduler)clazz.getMethod("instance",null).invoke(null,n
ull);
    }
  } catch (ClassNotFoundException notFound) {
  } catch (NoSuchMethodException noSuch) {
  } catch (SecurityException security) {
  } catch (IllegalAccessException access) {
  } catch (IllegalArgumentException arg) {
  } catch (InvocationTargetException target) {
  }
  return null;
}
```

To find, say, an EDF scheduler, the above method requires that the system property
javax.realtime.scheduler.EDF have been set to the fully qualified class name for
the EDF scheduler class. Thus, to get an EDF scheduler and use it to schedule a
periodic thread, t1, we do:

```
Scheduler scheduler = findScheduler("EDF");
if (scheduler != null) {
  RealtimeThread t1 =
    new RealtimeThread(
  null, /* default scheduling parameters */
  new PeriodicParameters(
    null, /*start immediately*/
    new RelativeTime(100, 0), /* period */
    new RelativeTime(5, 0), /* cost */
    new RelativeTime(50, 0), /* deadline */
    null,
    null),
  null,
  null,
  null) {
  public void run() {
    //thread processing
}
```

Once the scheduler is found, it is also possible to set it as the default scheduler for all subsequent thread creations. This is done with a call to Scheduler.setDefaultScheduler():

```
try {
  Scheduler.setDefaultScheduler(scheduler);
} catch (SecurityException security) {
};
```

Finally, you can test the current default scheduler to see if it implements the scheduling policy you want:

```
boolean useEDF = false;
try {
  if (Scheduler.getDefaultScheduler().getPolicyName().equals("EDF"
)) {
```

Life is grand, use EDF to your heart's content.

```
useEDF = true;
```

ProcessingGroup Example

Processing groups are used to provide information to the scheduler about aperiodic or sporadic activities — either threads or asynchronous event handlers — for the purposes of the feasibility analysis. The processing group carries information about the cost, period and deadline associated with aperiodic or sporadic activities that have been grouped together for the purposes of completing the analysis. The following will identify a processing group that allows for up to 10 milliseconds of execution during each 100 millisecond interval:

```
SchedulingParameters pp =
  new PriorityParameters(PriorityScheduler.getNormPriority());
ProcessingGroupParameters group =
  new ProcessingGroupParameters(null, /* start when released */
  new RelativeTime(100, 0), /* period */
  new RelativeTime(10, 0), /* cost */
  null, /* deadline == period */
  null, /* cost overrun handler */
  null); /* deadline miss handler */
```

Every thread that is created within this processing group should have a reference to the same processing group parameters object. The identity of the object is important to convey to the feasibility algorithm what group it is, in addition to the information about the group itself, so that the cost and period aren't accounted for more than once. Thus, after the first thread is added:

```
            RealtimeThread t1 = new RealtimeThread(
            pp, /* priority parameters */
            new AperiodicParameters(
       new RelativeTime(10,0), /* cost */
       new RelativeTime(300, 0), /* deadline */
       null, /* cost overrun handler */
       null), /* deadline miss handler */
            null, /* memory parameters */
            group,
            null) {
            public void run() {
            //do thread task
    }
```

We can add a second thread that goes in the same group:

```
       RealtimeThread t2 = new RealtimeThread(
            pp, /* priority parameters */
            new AperiodicParameters(
       new RelativeTime(5,0), /* cost */
       new RelativeTime(200, 0), /* deadline */
       null, /* cost overrun handler */
       null), /* deadline miss handler */
            null, /* memory parameters */
            group,
            null) {
            public void run() {
            //do thread task
    }
```

The priority of the `PriorityParameters` should be assigned according to the period of the processing group (relative to the periods of other periodic activities). This will affect both threads:

```
       sp.setPriority(GROUP_PRIORITY);
       t1.start();
       t2.start();
```

Both threads are now running. If the implementation can accumulate execution time per thread then, if either of these threads consumes more than 10ms in any period of this group, the cost overrun handler will be invoked. On the other hand, if the implementation cannot accumulate execution time per thread, then the deadline miss handler will be invoked if either thread is active at the end of the period of the group.

CHAPTER **5**

Memory Management

This section contains classes that:

- Allow the definition of regions of memory outside of the traditional Java heap.
- Allow the definition of regions of scoped memory, that is, memory regions with a limited lifetime.
- Allow the definition of regions of memory containing objects whose lifetime matches that of the application.
- Allow the definition of regions of memory mapped to specific physical addresses.
- Allow the specification of maximum memory area consumption and maximum allocation rates for individual real-time threads.
- Allow the programmer to query information characterizing the behavior of the garbage collection algorithm, and to some limited ability, alter the behavior of that algorithm.

Semantics and Requirements

The following list establishes the semantics and requirements that are applicable across the classes of this section. Semantics that apply to particular classes, constructors, methods, and fields will be found in the class description and the constructor, method, and field detail sections.

1. Some MemoryArea classes are required to have linear (in object size) allocation time. The linear time attribute requires that, ignoring performance variations due to hardware caches or similar optimizations and execution of any static initializers, the execution time of new must be bounded by a polynomial, f(n), where n is the size of the object and for all n>0, f(n) <= Cn for some constant C.

57

2. Execution time of object constructors is explicitly not considered in any bounds.

3. A memory scope is represented by an instance of the ScopedMemory class. When a new scope is entered, by calling the enter() method of the instance or by starting an instance of RealtimeThread or NoHeapRealtimeThread whose constructors were given a reference to an instance of ScopedMemory, all subsequent uses of the new keyword within the program logic of the scope will allocate the memory from the memory represented by that instance of ScopedMemory. When the scope is exited by returning from the enter() method of the instance of ScopedMemory, all subsequent uses of the new operation will allocate the memory from the area of memory associated with the enclosing scope.

4. Each instance of the class ScopedMemory or its subclasses must contain a reference count of the number of scopes in which it is being used.

5. The reference count for an instance of ScopedMemory or one of its subclasses is increased by one each time a reference to the instance is given to the constructor of a RealtimeThread or a NoHeapRealtimeThread, when a scope is opened for the instance (by calling the enter() method of the instance), and for each scope opened within its scope (whether for this instance or another instance).

6. The reference count for a ScopedMemory area is decreased by one when returning from an invocation of its enter() method, when an instance of RealtimeThread or NoHeapRealtimeThread to which the area is associated through a reference in the thread's MemoryParameters object exits, or when an inner scope returns from its enter() method (whether for this instance or another instance).

7. When the reference count for an instance of the class ScopedMemory or its subclasses is decremented from one to zero, all objects within that area are considered unreachable and as candidates for reclamation. The finalizers for each object in the memory associated with an instance of ScopedMemory are executed to completion before any statement in any thread attempts to access the memory area.

8. Scopes may be nested. When a nested scope is entered, all subsequent allocations are taken from the memory associated with the new scope. When the nested scope is exited, the previous scope is restored and subsequent allocations are again taken from that scope.

9. Any MemoryArea that is associated with a NoHeapRealtimeThread may not move any objects.

10. Objects created in any immortal memory area live for the duration of the application. The finalizers are only run when the application is terminated.

11. Each instance of the virtual machine will have exactly one instance of the class ImmortalMemory.

12. Each instance of the virtual machine will have exactly one instance of the class `HeapMemory`.

13. Each instance of the virtual machine will behave as if there is an area of memory into which all `Class` objects are placed and which is unexceptionally referenceable by `NoHeapRealtimeThreads`.

14. Strict assignment rules placed on assignments to or from memory areas prevent the creation of dangling pointers, and thus maintain the pointer safety of Java. The restrictions are listed in the following table:

	Reference to Heap	Reference to Immortal	Reference to Scoped
Heap	Yes	Yes	No
Immortal	Yes	Yes	No
Scoped	Yes	Yes	Yes, if same, outer, or shared scope
Local Variable	Yes	Yes	Yes, if same, outer, or shared scope

15. An implementation must ensure that the above checks are performed before the statement is executed. (This includes the possibility of static analysis of the application logic).

Rationale

Languages that employ automatic reclamation of blocks of memory allocated in what is traditionally called the heap by program logic also typically use an algorithm called a garbage collector. Garbage collection algorithms and implementations vary in the amount of non-determinancy they add to the execution of program logic. To date, the expert group believes that no garbage collector algorithm or implementation is known that allows preemption at points that leave the inter-object pointers in the heap in a consistent state and are sufficiently close in time to minimize the overhead added to task switch latencies to a sufficiently small enough value which could be considered appropriate for all real-time systems.

Thus, this specification provides the above described areas of memory to allow program logic to allocate objects in a Java-like style, ignore the reclamation of those objects, and not incur the latency of the implemented garbage collection algorithm.

5.1   MemoryArea

Syntax: `public abstract class MemoryArea`

Direct Known Subclasses: `HeapMemory`[61]`, ImmortalMemory`[62]`,`
`ImmortalPhysicalMemory`[69]`, ScopedMemory`[62]

`MemoryArea` is the abstract base class of all classes dealing with representations of allocatable memory areas, including the immortal memory area, physical memory and scoped memory areas.

5.1.1   Constructors

`protected `**`MemoryArea`**`(long sizeInBytes)`

> *Parameters:*
>> `sizeInBytes` - The size of the `MemoryArea` to allocate, in bytes.

5.1.2   Methods

`public void `**`enter`**`(java.lang.Runnable logic)`
> Associate this memory area to the current real-time thread for the duration of the execution of the `run()` method of the given `java.lang.Runnable`. During this bound period of execution, all objects are allocated from the memory area until another one takes effect, or the `enter()` method is exited. A runtime exception is thrown if this method is called from thread other than a `RealtimeThread`[22] or `NoHeapRealtimeThread`[26].

> *Parameters:*
>> `logic` - The runnable object whose `run()` method should be executed.

`public static MemoryArea`[60] **`getMemoryArea`**`(java.lang.Object object)`
> Return the `MemoryArea` in which the given object is located.

`public long `**`memoryConsumed`**`()`
> An exact count, in bytes, of the all of the memory currently used by the system for the allocated objects.

> *Returns:* The amount of memory consumed in bytes.

`public long `**`memoryRemaining`**`()`
> An approximation to the total amount of memory currently available for future allocated objects, measured in bytes.

> *Returns:* The amount of remaining memory in bytes.

```
public synchronized java.lang.Object newArray(java.lang.Class type,
                       int number)
```
Allocate an array of T in this memory area.

Parameters:
> `type` - The class of the elements of the new array.
> `number` - The number of elements in the new array.

Returns: A new array of class `type`, of `number` elements.

Throws: `IllegalAccessException` - The class or initializer is inaccessible.
> `InstantiationException` - The array cannot be instantiated.
> `OutOfMemoryError` - Space in the memory area is exhausted.

```
public synchronized java.lang.Object newInstance(java.lang.Class
                       type)
```
Allocate an object in this memory area.

Parameters:
> `type` - The class of which to create a new instance.

Returns: A new instance of class `type`.

Throws: `IllegalAccessException` - The class or initializer is inaccessible.
> `InstantiationException` - The specified class object could not be instantiated. Possible causes are: it is an interface, it is abstract, it is an array, or an exception was thrown by the constructor.
> `OutOfMemoryError` - Space in the memory area is exhausted.

```
public long size()
```
Query the size of the memory area. The returned value is the current size. Current size may be larger than initial size for those areas that are allowed to grow.

Returns: The size of the memory area in bytes.

5.2 HeapMemory

Syntax: `public final class HeapMemory extends MemoryArea`$_{60}$

The `HeapMemory` class is a singleton object that allows logic within other scoped memory to allocate objects in the Java heap.

5.2.1   Methods

`public static HeapMemory`$_{61}$ `instance()`
    Return a pointer to the singleton `HeapMemory` space

    Returns: The singleton `HeapMemory` object.

5.3   ImmortalMemory

Syntax: `public final class ImmortalMemory extends MemoryArea`$_{60}$

    `ImmortalMemory` is a memory resource that is shared among all threads. Objects allocated in the immortal memory live until the end of the application. Objects in immortal memory are never subject to garbage collection, although some GC algorithms may require a scan of the immortal memory. An *immortal* object may only contain reference to other immortal objects or to heap objects. Unlike standard Java heap objects, immortal objects continue to exist even after there are no other references to them.

5.3.1   Methods

`public static ImmortalMemory`$_{62}$ `instance()`
    Return a pointer to the singleton `ImmortalMemory` space.

5.4   ScopedMemory

Syntax: `public abstract class ScopedMemory extends MemoryArea`$_{60}$

Direct Known Subclasses: `LTMemory`$_{65}$, `ScopedPhysicalMemory`$_{71}$, `VTMemory`$_{65}$

    `ScopedMemory` is the abstract base class of all classes dealing with representations of memory spaces with a limited lifetime. The `ScopedMemory` area is valid as long as there are real-time threads with access to it. A reference is created for each accessor when either a real-time thread is created with the `ScopedMemory` object as its memory area, or a real-time thread runs the `public void enter(java.lang.Runnable logic)`$_{64}$ method for the memory area. When the last reference to the object is removed, by exiting the thread or exiting the `enter()` method, finalizers are run for all objects in the memory area, and the area is emptied.

    A `ScopedMemory` area is a connection to a particular region of memory and reflects the current status of it. The object does not necessarily contain direct references to the region of memory that is implementation dependent.

When a ScopedMemory area is instantiated, the object itself is allocated from the current memory allocation scheme in use, but the memory space that object represents is not. Typically, the memory for a ScopedMemory area might be allocated using native method implementations that make appropriate use of `malloc()` and `free()` or similar routines to manipulate memory. The `enter()` method of ScopedMemory is the mechanism used to activate a new memory scope. Entry into the scope is done by calling the method:

```
public void enter(Runnable r)
```

Where *r* is a Runnable object whose `run()` method represents the entry point to the code that will run in the new scope. Exit from the scope occurs when the `r.run()` completes. Allocations of objects within `r.run()` are done with the ScopedMemory area. When `r.run()` is complete, the scoped memory area is no longer active. Its reference count will be decremented and if it is zero all of the objects in the memory area finalized and collected.

Objects allocated from a ScopedMemory area have a unique lifetime. They cease to exist on exiting a `public void enter(java.lang.Runnable logic)`$_{64}$ method or upon exiting the last real-time thread referencing the area, regardless of any references that may exist to the object. Thus, to maintain the safety of Java and avoid dangling references, a very restrictive set of rules apply to ScopedMemory area objects:

1. A reference to an object in ScopedMemory can never be stored in an Object allocated in the Java heap.

2. A reference to an object in ScopedMemory can never be stored in an Object allocated in ImmortalMemory$_{62}$.

3. A reference to an object in ScopedMemory can only be stored in Objects allocated in the same ScopedMemory area, or into a — more inner — ScopedMemory area nested by the use of its `enter()` method.

4. References to immortal or heap objects *may* be stored into an object allocated in a ScopedMemory area.

5.4.1   Constructors

`public ScopedMemory(long size)`
   Create a new ScopedMemory area with a particular size.

   Parameters:
      `size` - The size of the new ScopedMemory area in bytes. If size is less than or equal to zero nothing happens.

5.4.2   Methods

public void **enter**(java.lang.Runnable logic)

> Associate this ScopedMemory area to the current real-time thread for the duration of the execution of the run() method of the given java.lang.Runnable . During this bound period of execution, all objects are allocated from the ScopedMemory area until another one takes effect, or the enter() method is exited. A runtime exception is thrown if this method is called from a thread other than a $RealtimeThread_{22}$ or $NoHeapRealtimeThread_{26}$.

> *Overrides:* public void enter(java.lang.Runnable logic)$_{60}$ in class $MemoryArea_{60}$

> *Parameters:*
>> logic - The runnable object which contains the code to execute.

public int **getMaximumSize**()

> Get the maximum size this memory area can attain. If this is a fixed size memory area, the returned value will be equal to the initial size.

public $MemoryArea_{60}$ **getOuterScope**()

> Find the ScopedMemory area in effect, for the current $RealtimeThread_{22}$, prior to the current invocation of a ScopedMemoryenter} method.

> *Returns:* The containing scope. If this is the outermost scoped memory then the $MemoryArea_{60}$ associated with the thread.

public java.lang.Object **getPortal**()

> Return a reference to the portal object in this instance of ScopedMemory.

> *Returns:* The portal object or null if there is no portal object.

public void **setPortal**(java.lang.Object object)

> Set the argument to the portal object in the memory area represented by this instance of ScopedMemory.

> *Parameters:*
>> object - The object which will become the portal for this. If null the previous portal object remains the portal object for this or if there was no previous portal object then there is still no portal object for this.

5.5 VTMemory

Syntax: public class VTMemory extends ScopedMemory$_{62}$

The execution time of an allocation from a VTMemory area may take a variable amount of time. However, since VTMemory areas are not subject to garbage collection and objects within may not be moved, these areas can be used by instances of NoHeapRealtimeThread$_{26}$.

5.5.1 Constructors

public **VTMemory**(int initial, intmaximum)
Create a VTMemory of the given size.

Parameters:
initial - The size in bytes of the memory to initially allocate for this area.
maximum - The maximum size in bytes this memory area can grow to.

5.6 LTMemory

Syntax: public class LTMemory extends ScopedMemory$_{62}$

LTMemory represents a memory area, allocated per RealtimeThread$_{22}$, or for a group of real-time threads, guaranteed by the system to have linear time allocation. The memory area described by a LTMemory instance does not exist in the Java heap, and is not subject to garbage collection. Thus, it is safe to use a LTMemory object as the memory area associated with a NoHeapRealtimeThread$_{26}$, or to enter the memory area using the public void enter(java.lang.Runnable logic)$_{64}$ method within a NoHeapRealtimeThread$_{26}$. An LTMemory area has an initial size. Enough memory must be committed by the completion of the constructor to satisfy this initial requirement. (Committed means that this memory must always be available for allocation). The initial memory allocation must behave, with respect to successful allocation, as if it were contiguous; i.e., a correct implementation must guarantee that any sequence of object allocations that could ever succeed without exceeding a specified initial memory size will always succeed without exceeding that initial memory size and succeed for any instance of LTMemory with that initial memory size. *(Note: It is important to understand that the above statement does **not require that if the initial memory size is N and (sizeof(object1) + sizeof(object2) + ... + sizeof(objectn) = N) the allocations of objects 1 through n will necessarily succeed.)** Execution time of an allocator allocating from this initial area must be linear in the size of the allocated object. Execution time of an allocator allocating from memory between initial and maximum is allowed to vary. Furthermore, the underlying system is not required to guarantee that memory between initial and maximum will always be available. (Note: to ensure that all requested memory is available set inital and maximum to the same value) See also: MemoryArea$_{60}$ ScopedMemory$_{62}$ RealtimeThread$_{22}$ NoHeapRealtimeThread$_{26}$

5.6.1   Constructors

public **LTMemory**(long initialSizeInBytes, longmaxSizeInBytes)
> Create a LTMemory of the given size.

> *Parameters:*
>> initialSizeInBytes - The size in bytes of the memory to allocate for this area. This memory must be committed before the completion of the constructor.
>> maxSizeInBytes - The size in bytes of the memory to allocate for this area.

ScopedMemory Example

A real-time thread — including the primordial thread will perform allocations from within the memory area assigned to the thread. The default memory area is the Java heap. Allocations can be performed from a different memory area in one of two ways: entering a new scope, or calling newInstance() or newArray() on a different memory area. To enter a new scope that has constant time allocation:

```
final ScopedMemory scope = new CTMemory(16 * 1024);
```

The enter() method will call the run method of the given object with memory area as the object pool for allocations. All new operations will come from the constant-time pool until a new scope is entered, or the run() method completes.

```
scope.enter(new Runnable() {
  public void run() {
    //do some time-critical operations
    //to allocate from the heap within this scope:
    try {
        HeapMemory.instance().newInstance(Class.forName("Foo"));
        //to allocate from the previous scope within this one
        scope.getOuterScope().newInstance(Class.forName("Foo"));
    } catch (ClassNotFoundException e) {
    } catch (IllegalAccessException ia) {
    } catch (InstantiationException ie) {
    }}});
```

ScopedMemory Example 2

A real-time thread may be associated with a memory area when it is created. All new operations will allocate objects for the thread from the object pool provided by the memory area.

```
final ScopedMemory scope = new CTMemory(16 * 1024);
RealtimeThread t1 = new RealtimeThread(null, null,
  new MemoryParameters(scope), null,
  new Runnable() {
 public void run() {
   //do some stuff
}
```

Additional threads can share the same memory area, and the reference count will be incremented.

```
RealtimeThread t2 = new RealtimeThread(null, null,
  new MemoryParameters(scope), null,
  new Runnable() {
 public void run() {
   //do some other stuff
}
```

Wait for the threads to finish

```
boolean interrupted = false;
do {
  try {
    t1.join();
  } catch (InterruptedException ie) {
    interrupted = true;
  }
} while (interrupted);
interrupted = false;
do {
  try {
    t2.join();
  } catch (InterruptedException ie) {
    interrupted = true;
  }
} while (interrupted);
```

After this point, the threads are dead, and the reference count will have dropped to zero so finalizers **may** be run. If we now try to create a new thread using the memory area:

```
RealtimeThread t3 = new RealtimeThread(null, null,
  new MemoryParameters(scope), null,
  new Runnable() {
 public void run() {
    //do some other stuff
 }
```

The constructor will block until the finalizers have completed. It will then be safe to start the thread:

```
    t3.start();
```

5.7   PhysicalMemoryFactory

Syntax: `public class PhysicalMemoryFactory`

The `PhysicalMemoryFactory` is available for use by the various physical memory accessor objects to create objects of the correct type that are bound to areas of physical memory with the appropriate characteristics — or with appropriate accessor behavior. Examples of characteristics that might be specified are: DMA memory, accessors with byte swapping, etc. The implementation will provide a default factory. OEMs may provide derived factories that allow additional characteristics to be specified.

5.7.1   Fields

`public static final java.lang.String ALIGNED`
  Specify this to identify aligned memory.

`public static final java.lang.String BYTESWAP`
  Specify this if byte swapping should be used.

`public static final java.lang.String DMA`
  Specify this to identify DMA memory.

`public static final java.lang.String SHARED`
  Specify this to identify shared memory.

5.7.2　Methods

```
protected synchronized java.lang.Object create(java.lang.Object
            memoryType, java.lang.ClassphysMemType,
            long base, longsize)
```
Used to actually create the physical memory accessor.

Parameters:
> memoryType - Description of the memory type required.
> physMemType - Indicates the type of physical memory object to
>   construct.
> base - The physical address of the start of the region.
> size - The size of the region in bytes.

```
protected synchronized long getTypedMemoryBase(java.lang.Object
            memoryType, longsize)
```
Get the base address of a range of memory of the correct type that is at least the size specified.

Parameters:
> size - The desired size of the memory range.

5.8　ImmortalPhysicalMemory

Syntax: `public class ImmortalPhysicalMemory extends MemoryArea`$_{60}$

An instance of `ImmortalPhysicalMemory` allows objects to be allocated from a range of physical memory with particular attributes, determined by their *memory type*. This memory area has the same restrictive set of assignment rules as `ImmortalMemory`$_{62}$ memory areas and may be used in any constructor where `ImmortalMemory`$_{62}$ is appropriate. Objects allocated in immortal physical memory have a lifetime greater than the application as do objects allocated in immortal memory.

5.8.1　Constructors

```
protected ImmortalPhysicalMemory(ImmortalPhysicalMemory69 memory,
            long base, longsize)
```
Constructor for use by the memory object factory.

```
protected ImmortalPhysicalMemory(long base, long size)
```

5.8.2   Methods

`public static ImmortalPhysicalMemory`$_{69}$ **`create`**`(java.lang.Object`
`                type, long size)`

Parameters:

> `type` - An object representing the type of memory required (e.g.,
> *dma, shared*) - used to define the base address and control the
> mapping. The passed object is typically provided by the vendor
> of the physical memory or the implementation vendor.
> `size` - The size of the memory area in bytes.

Throws: `SecurityException` - The application doesn't have permissions
> to access physical memory or the given type of memory.
> `SizeOutOfBoundsException`$_{156}$ - The size is negative or extends
> into an invalid range of memory.
> `UnsupportedPhysicalMemoryException`$_{157}$ - Thrown if the
> underlying hardware does not support the given type.

`public static ImmortalPhysicalMemory`$_{69}$ **`create`**`(java.lang.Object`
`                type, long base, long size)`

Parameters:

> `type` - An object representing the type of memory required (e.g.,
> *dma, shared*). The passed object is typically provided by the
> vendor of the physical memory or the implementation vendor.
> `base` - The physical memory address of the region
> `size` - The size of the memory area in bytes.

Throws: `SecurityException` - The application doesn't have permissions
> to access physical memory or the given range of memory.
> `OffsetOutOfBoundsException`$_{155}$ - The address is invalid.
> `SizeOutOfBoundsException`$_{156}$ - The size is negative or extends
> into an invalid range of memory.
> `UnsupportedPhysicalMemoryException`$_{157}$ - Thrown if the
> underlying hardware does not support the given type.

`public static void` **`setFactory`**`(PhysicalMemoryFactory`$_{68}$ `factory)`
Set the physical memory factory to the given argument.

Parameters:

> `factory` - A physical memory factory which will be the factory for
> `PhysicalMemoryFactory`$_{68}$ at the completion of this method.

5.9   ScopedPhysicalMemory

Syntax: `public class ScopedPhysicalMemory extends ScopedMemory`$_{62}$

An instance of `ScopedPhysicalMemory` allows objects to be allocated from a range of physical memory with particular attributes, determined by their memory type. This memory area has the same restrictive set of assignment rules as `ScopedMemory`$_{62}$ memory areas.

5.9.1   Constructors

protected **ScopedPhysicalMemory**(long base, lo n gsize)
> Constructor for use by the memory object factory.

protected **ScopedPhysicalMemory**(ScopedPhysicalMemory$_{71}$ memory,
>   long base, longsize)
> Constructor for use by the memory object factory.

5.9.2   Methods

public static ScopedPhysicalMemory$_{71}$ **create**(java.lang.Object type,
>   long base, longsize)

> *Parameters:*
>> type - An Object representing the type of memory required (e.g., *dma, shared*)
>> base - The physical memory address of the area.
>> size - The size of the area in bytes.

> *Throws:* SecurityException - The application doesn't have permissions to access physical memory or the given range of memory.
>> OffsetOutOfBoundsException$_{155}$ - The address is invalid.
>> SizeOutOfBoundsException$_{156}$ - The size is negative or extends into an invalid range of memory.
>> UnsupportedPhysicalMemoryException$_{157}$ - Thrown if the underlying hardware does not support the given type.

public static void **setFactory**(PhysicalMemoryFactory$_{68}$ factory)
> Sets the factory that will be used to generate ScopedPhysicalMemory instances.

> *Parameters:*
>> factory - The PhysicalMemoryFactory$_{68}$ which will become the factory for this. If null the previous factory remains as the factory for this.

5.10 RawMemoryAccess

Syntax: `public class RawMemoryAccess`

Direct Known Subclasses: `RawMemoryFloatAccess`$_{76}$

An instance of `RawMemoryAccess` models a range of physical memory as a fixed-size sequence of bytes. A full complement of accessor methods allow the contents of the physical memory area to be accessed through offsets from the base, interpreted as byte, short, int, or long data values or as arrays of these types.

Whether the offset addresses the high-order or low-order byte is based on the value of the BYTE_ORDER static boolean variable in class `RealtimeSystem`$_{150}$.

The `RawMemoryAccess` class allows a real-time program to implement device drivers, memory-mapped I/O, flash memory, battery-backed RAM, and similar low-level software.

A raw memory area cannot contain references to Java objects. Such a capability would be unsafe (since it could be used to defeat Java's type checking) and error-prone (since it is sensitive to the specific representational choices made by the Java compiler).

Many of the constructors and methods in this class throw `OffsetOutOfBoundsException`$_{155}$. This exception means that the value given in the offset parameter is either negative or outside the memory area.

Many of the constructors and methods in this class throw `SizeOutOfBoundsException`$_{156}$. This exception means that the value given in the size parameter is either negative, larger than an allowable range, or would cause an accessor method to access an address outside of the memory area.

5.10.1 Constructors

protected **RawMemoryAccess**(`long base, longsize`)

protected **RawMemoryAccess**(`RawMemoryAccess`$_{72}$ `memory, long base, long size`)
    Constructor reserved for use by the memory object factory.

5.10.2 Methods

public static RawMemoryAccess$_{72}$ **create**(`java.lang.Object type, long size`)

Parameters:

> type - An Object representing the type of memory required (e.g.,
> *dma, shared*) - used to define the base address and control the
> mapping
> size - The size of the area in bytes.

Throws: SecurityException - The application doesn't have permissions
to access physical memory or the given type of memory.
OffsetOutOfBoundsException$_{155}$ - The address is invalid.
SizeOutOfBoundsException$_{156}$ - The size is negative or extends
into an invalid range of memory.
UnsupportedPhysicalMemoryException$_{157}$ - Thrown if the
underlying hardware does not support the given type.

public static RawMemoryAccess$_{72}$ **create**(java.lang.Object type,
                long base, longsize)

Parameters:

> type - An Object representing the type of memory required (e.g.,
> *dma, shared*)
> base - The physical memory address of the region
> size - The size of the area in bytes.

Throws: SecurityException - The application doesn't have permissions
to access physical memory or the given range of memory.
OffsetOutOfBoundsException$_{155}$ - The address is invalid.
SizeOutOfBoundsException$_{156}$ - The size is negative or extends
into an invalid range of memory.
UnsupportedPhysicalMemoryException$_{157}$ - Thrown if the
underlying hardware does not support the given type.

public byte **getByte**(long offset)
Get the byte at the given offset.

Throws: SizeOutOfBoundsException$_{156}$,
OffsetOutOfBoundsException$_{155}$

public void **getBytes**(long offset, byte[]bytes, intlow,
                int number)
Get number bytes starting at the given offset in this and assign them into the
byte array starting at position low.

Throws: SizeOutOfBoundsException$_{156}$,
OffsetOutOfBoundsException$_{155}$

public int **getInt**(long offset)
Get the int at the given offset.

Throws: SizeOutOfBoundsException$_{156}$,
          OffsetOutOfBoundsException$_{155}$

public void **getInts**(long offset, int[] ints, int low, i n tnumber)
   Get number int values, starting at the given offset in this, and assign
   them into the int array starting at position low.

Throws: SizeOutOfBoundsException$_{156}$,
          OffsetOutOfBoundsException$_{155}$

public long **getLong**(long offset)
   Get the long value at the given offset.

Throws: SizeOutOfBoundsException$_{156}$,
          OffsetOutOfBoundsException$_{155}$

public void **getLongs**(long offset, long[]longs, intlow,
                    int number)
   Get number long values, starting at the given offset in this, and assign
   them into the long array starting at position low.

Throws: SizeOutOfBoundsException$_{156}$,
          OffsetOutOfBoundsException$_{155}$

public long **getMappedAddress**()
   Return the virtual memory location at which the memory region is mapped.

Returns: The virtual address to which this is mapped (for reference
           purposes). Same as the base address if virtual memory isn't
           supported.

public short **getShort**(long offset)
   Get the short at the given offset.

Throws: SizeOutOfBoundsException$_{156}$,
          OffsetOutOfBoundsException$_{155}$

public void **getShorts**(long offset, short[]shorts, intlow,
                     int number)
   Get number shorts starting at the given offset in this from the short array
   starting at position low.

Throws: SizeOutOfBoundsException$_{156}$,
          OffsetOutOfBoundsException$_{155}$

public long **map**()
   Map the physical address range into virtual memory. No-op if the system
   doesn't support virtual memory.

Returns: The virtual address to which this is mapped (for reference
           purposes).

```
public long map(long base)
```
Map the physical address range into virtual memory at the specified location. No-op if the system doesn't support virtual memory.

Parameters:
> base - The location to map to in the virtual address space.

Returns: The virtual address to which this is mapped (for reference purposes).

```
public long map(long base, longsize)
```
Map the physical address range into virtual memory at the specified location. No-op if the system doesn't support virtual memory.

Parameters:
> base - The location to map to in the virtual address space.
> size - The size of the block to map in.

Returns: The virtual address to which this is mapped (for reference purposes).

```
public void setByte(long offset, byte value)
```
Set the byte at the given offset.

Throws: SizeOutOfBoundsException$_{156}$, OffsetOutOfBoundsException$_{155}$

```
public void setBytes(long offset, byte[]bytes, intlow,
                  int number)
```
Set number bytes starting at the given offset in this from the byte array starting at position low.

Throws: SizeOutOfBoundsException$_{156}$, OffsetOutOfBoundsException$_{155}$

```
public void setInt(long offset, i n tvalue)
```
Set the int value at the given offset.

Throws: SizeOutOfBoundsException$_{156}$, OffsetOutOfBoundsException$_{155}$

```
public void setInts(long offset, int[] ints, int low, i n tnumber)
```
Set number int values starting at the given offset in this, from the int array starting at position low.

Throws: SizeOutOfBoundsException$_{156}$, OffsetOutOfBoundsException$_{155}$

```
public void setLong(long offset, long value)
```
Set the long value at the given offset starting at position low.

Throws: SizeOutOfBoundsException$_{156}$,
         OffsetOutOfBoundsException$_{155}$

public void **setLongs**(long offset, long[]longs, intlow ,   intn)
Set number long values starting at the given offset in this, from the long array starting at position low.

Throws: SizeOutOfBoundsException$_{156}$,
         OffsetOutOfBoundsException$_{155}$

public void **setShort**(long offset, shortvalue)
Set the short at the given offset.

Throws: SizeOutOfBoundsException$_{156}$,
         OffsetOutOfBoundsException$_{155}$

public void **setShorts**(long offset, short[]shorts, intlow,
                 int number)
Set number shorts starting at the given offset in this, from the short array starting at position low.

Throws: SizeOutOfBoundsException$_{156}$,
         OffsetOutOfBoundsException$_{155}$

public void **unmap**()
Unmap the physical address range from virtual memory. No-op if the system doesn't support virtual memory.

5.11   RawMemoryFloatAccess

Syntax: public class RawMemoryFloatAccess extends RawMemoryAccess$_{72}$

This class holds the accessor methods for accessing a raw memory area by float and double types. Implementations are required to implement this class if and only if the underlying Java Virtual Machine supports floating point data types.

Many of the constructors and methods in this class throw OffsetOutOfBoundsException$_{155}$. This exception means that the value given in the offset parameter is either negative or outside the memory area.

Many of the constructors and methods in this class throw SizeOutOfBoundsException$_{156}$. This exception means that the value given in the size parameter is either negative, larger than an allowable range, or would cause an accessor method to access an address outside of the memory area.

5.11.1 Constructors

protected **RawMemoryFloatAccess**(long base, lo n gsize)

protected **RawMemoryFloatAccess**(RawMemoryAccess$_{72}$ memory, long base,
long size)
Constructor reserved for use by the memory object factory.

5.11.2 Methods

public static RawMemoryFloatAccess$_{76}$
createFloatAccess(java.lang.Object type,
long size)

Parameters:
type - An Object representing the type of memory required (e.g.,
dma, shared) - used to define the base address and control the
mapping
size - The size of the area in bytes.

Throws: SecurityException - The application doesn't have permissions
to access physical memory or the given type of memory.
OffsetOutOfBoundsException$_{155}$ - The address is invalid.
SizeOutOfBoundsException$_{156}$ - The size is negative or extends
into an invalid range of memory.
UnsupportedPhysicalMemoryException$_{157}$ - Thrown if the
underlying hardware does not support the given type.

public static RawMemoryFloatAccess$_{76}$
createFloatAccess(java.lang.Object type,
long base, longsize)

Parameters:
type - An Object representing the type of memory required (e.g.,
dma, shared)
base - The physical memory address of the area.
size - The size of the area in bytes.

Throws: SecurityException - The application doesn't have permissions
to access physical memory or the given range of memory.
OffsetOutOfBoundsException$_{155}$ - The address is invalid.
SizeOutOfBoundsException$_{156}$ - The size is negative or extends
into an invalid range of memory.
UnsupportedPhysicalMemoryException$_{157}$ - Thrown if the
underlying hardware does not support the given type.

public byte **getDouble**(long offset)
Get the double at the given offset.

Throws: SizeOutOfBoundsException$_{156}$,
          OffsetOutOfBoundsException$_{155}$

public void **getDoubles**(long offset, double[]doubless, in tlow,
                int number)
Get number double values starting at the given offset in this, and assigns
them into the double array starting at position low.

Throws: SizeOutOfBoundsException$_{156}$,
          OffsetOutOfBoundsException$_{155}$

public byte **getFloat**(long offset)
Get the float at the given offset.

Throws: SizeOutOfBoundsException$_{156}$,
          OffsetOutOfBoundsException$_{155}$

public void **getFloats**(long offset, float[]floats, intlow,
                int number)
Get number float values starting at the given offset in this and assign
them into the byte array starting at position low.

Throws: SizeOutOfBoundsException$_{156}$,
          OffsetOutOfBoundsException$_{155}$

public void **setDouble**(long offset, doublevalue)
Set the double at the given offset.

Throws: SizeOutOfBoundsException$_{156}$,
          OffsetOutOfBoundsException$_{155}$

public void **setDoubles**(long offset, double[]doubles ,   intlow,
                int number)
Set number double values starting at the given offset in this, from the
double array starting at position low.

Throws: SizeOutOfBoundsException$_{156}$,
          OffsetOutOfBoundsException$_{155}$

public void **setFloat**(long offset, floatvalue)
Set the float at the given offset.

Throws: SizeOutOfBoundsException$_{156}$,
          OffsetOutOfBoundsException$_{155}$

public void **setFloats**(long offset, float[]floats, intlow,
                int number)
Set number float values starting at the given offset in this from the byte
array starting at position low.

Throws: `SizeOutOfBoundsException`$_{156}$,
`OffsetOutOfBoundsException`$_{155}$

5.12 MemoryParameters

Syntax: `public class MemoryParameters`

Memory parameters can be given on the constructor of `RealtimeThread`$_{22}$ and `AsyncEventHandler`$_{127}$. These can be used both for the purposes of admission control by the scheduler and for the purposes of pacing the garbage collector to satisfy all of the thread allocation rates. When a reference to a `MemoryParameters` object is given as a parameter to a constructor, the `MemoryParameters` object becomes bound to the object being created. Changes to the values in the `MemoryParameters` object affect the constructed object. If given to more than one constructor, then changes to the values in the `MemoryParameters` object affect *all* of the associated objects. Note that this is a one-to-many relationship and *not* a many-to-many.

Caution: This class is explicitly unsafe in multithreaded situations when it is being changed. No synchronization is done. It is assumed that users of this class who are mutating instances will be doing their own synchronization at a higher level.

5.12.1 Fields

`public static final long NO_MAX`

5.12.2 Constructors

`public MemoryParameters(long maxMemoryArea, longmaxImmortal)`
Create a `MemoryParameters` object with the given values.

Parameters:
`maxMemoryArea` - A limit on the amount of memory the thread may allocate in the memory area. Units are in bytes. If zero, no allocation allowed in the memory area. To specify no limit, use NO_MAX or a value less than zero.
`maxImmortal` - A limit on the amount of memory the thread may allocate in the immortal area. Units are in bytes. If zero, no allocation allowed in immortal. To specify no limit, use NO_MAX or a value less than zero.

Throws: `IllegalArgumentException`

public **MemoryParameters**(long maxMemoryArea, longmaxImmortal,
              long allocationRate)
Create a MemoryParameters object with the given values.

Parameters:
> maxMemoryArea - A limit on the amount of memory the thread may
> allocate in the memory area. Units are in bytes. If zero, no
> allocation allowed in the memory area. To specify no limit, use
> NO_MAX or a value less than zero.
> maxImmortal - A limit on the amount of memory the thread may
> allocate in the immortal area. Units are in bytes. If zero, no
> allocation allowed in immortal. To specify no limit, use
> NO_MAX or a value less than zero.
> allocationRate - A limit on the rate of allocation in the heap. Units
> are in bytes per second. If zero, no allocation is allowed in the
> heap. To specify no limit, use NO_MAX or a value less than
> zero.

Throws: IllegalArgumentException

5.12.3 Methods

public long **getAllocationRate**()
Get the allocation rate. Units are bytes per second.

public long **getMaxImmortal**()
Get the limit on the amount of memory the thread may allocate in the
immortal area. Units are in bytes.

public long **getMaxMemoryArea**()
Get the limit on the amount of memory the thread may allocate in the
memory area. Units are in bytes.

public void **setAllocationRate**(long rate)
A limit on the rate of allocation in the heap.

Parameters:
> rate - Units are in bytes per second. If zero, no allocation is allowed
> in the heap. To specify no limit, use NO_MAX or a value less
> than zero.

```
public boolean setMaxImmortal(long maximum)
```
Set the limit on the amount of memory the thread may allocate in the immortal area.

Parameters:
> `maximum` - Units are in bytes. If zero, no allocation is allowed in the immortal area. To specify no limit, use NO_MAX or a value less than zero.

Returns: False if any of the threads have already allocated more than the given value. In this case the call has no effect.

```
public boolean setMaxMemoryArea(long maximum)
```
Set the limit on the amount of memory the thread may allocate in the memory area.

Parameters:
> `maximum` - Units are in bytes. If zero, no allocation allowed in the memory area. To specify no limit, use NO_MAX or a value less than zero.

Returns: False if any of the threads have already allocated more than the given value. In this case the call has no effect.

5.13 GarbageCollector

Syntax: `public abstract class GarbageCollector`

Direct Known Subclasses: IncrementalCollectorExample$_{82}$, MarkAndSweepCollectorExample$_{83}$

The system shall provide dynamic and static information characterizing the temporal behavior and imposed overhead of any garbage collection algorithm provided by the system. This impormation shall be made available to applications via methods on subclasses of GarbageCollector. Implementations are allowed to provide any set of methods in subclasses as long as the temporal behavior and overhead are sufficiently categorized. The implementations are also required to fully document the subclasses. In addition, the method(s) in GarbageCollector shall be made available by all implementations. See: IncrementalCollectorExample$_{82}$ and MarkAndSweepCollectorExample$_{83}$

5.13.1 Constructors

public **GarbageCollector**()

5.13.2 Methods

public abstract RelativeTime$_{102}$ **getPreemptionLatency**()
Instances of RealtimeThread$_{22}$ are allowed to preempt the execution of the garbage collector (instances of NoHeapRealtimeThread$_{26}$ preempt immediately but instances of RealtimeThread$_{22}$ must wait until the collector reaches a preemption-safe point). Preemption latency is a measure of the maximum time a RealtimeThread$_{22}$ may have to wait for the collector to reach a preemption-safe point.

Returns: The preempting latency of this if applicable. May return zero if there is no collector avaiable.

5.14 IncrementalCollectorExample

Syntax: public class IncrementalCollectorExample extends GarbageCollector$_{81}$

This class is provided as an example only and is not required on any implementation, even ones which employ an incremental collector.

5.14.1 Constructors

public **IncrementalCollectorExample**()

5.14.2 Methods

public long **getMaximumReclamationRate**()
Maximum reclamation rate the garbage collector can sustain. This is a dynamically assigned value dependent on schedule.

Returns: Return value is measured in kilobytes per second.

public RelativeTime$_{102}$ **getPreemptionLatency**()
The instantiation of the abstract method in GarbageCollector.

Overrides: public abstract RelativeTime102 getPreemptionLatency()$_{82}$ in class GarbageCollector$_{81}$

public int **getReadBarrierOverhead**()
> Overhead of the read barrier. Given in percentage of the cost of a field access.

public int **getWriteBarrierOverhead**()
> Overhead of the write barrier. Given in percentage of the cost of an assignment.

public void **setReclamationRate**(int rate)
> The reclamation rate as a ratio: 1 / number of kilobytes scanned per kilobyte allocated. Used by incremental collection algorithms to pace their reclamation rate.

> *Parameters:*
>> rate - The new reclamation rate. Ignored if collector does not

---

5.15 MarkAndSweepCollectorExample

Syntax: public class MarkAndSweepCollectorExample extends GarbageCollector$_{81}$

This class is provided as an example only and is not required on any implementation, even ones which employ an incremental collector.

5.15.1 Constructors

public **MarkAndSweepCollectorExample**()

5.15.2 Methods

public RelativeTime$_{102}$ **getPreemptionLatency**()
> The instantiation of the abstract method in GarbageCollector.

> *Overrides:* public abstract RelativeTime102
>> getPreemptionLatency()$_{82}$ in class GarbageCollector$_{81}$

CHAPTER **6**

Synchronization

This section contains classes that:

- Allow the application of the priority ceiling emulation algorithm to individual objects.
- Allow the setting of the system default priority inversion algorithm.
- Allow wait-free communication between real-time threads and regular Java threads.

The specification strengthens the semantics of Java synchronization for use in real-time systems by mandating monitor execution eligibility control, commonly referred to as priority inversion control. A MonitorControl class is defined as the superclass of all such execution eligibility control algorithms. PriorityInheritance is the default monitor control policy; the specification also defines a PriorityCeilingEmulation option.

The wait-free queue classes provide protected, concurrent access to data shared between instances of java.lang.Thread and NoHeapRealtimeThread.

Semantics and Requirements

This list establishes the semantics and requirements that are applicable across the classes of this section. Semantics that apply to particular classes, constructors, methods, and fields will be found in the class description and the constructor, method, and field detail sections.

1. Threads waiting to enter synchronized blocks are priority queue ordered. If threads with the same priority are possible under the active scheduling policy such threads are queued in FIFO order.

2. Any conforming implementation must provide an implementation of the synchronized primitive with default behavior that ensures that there is no unbounded priority inversion. Furthermore, this must apply to code if it is run within the implementation as well as to real-time threads.

3. The Priority Inheritance monitor control policy must be implemented.

4. Implementations that provide a monitor control algorithm in addition to those described herein are required to clearly document the behavior of that algorithm.

Rationale

Java monitors, and especially the synchronized keyword, provide a very elegant means for mutual exclusion synchronization. Thus, rather than invent a new real-time synchronization mechanism, this specification strengthens the semantics of Java synchronization to allow its use in real-time systems. In particular, this specification mandates priority inversion control. Priority inheritance and priority ceiling emulation are both popular priority inversion control mechanisms; however, priority inheritance is more widely implemented in real-time operating systems and so is the default mechanism in this specification.

By design the only mechanism required by this specification which can enforce mutual exclusion in the traditional sense is the keyword synchronized. Noting that the specification allows the use of synchronized by both instances of java.lang.Thread, RealtimeThread, and NoHeapRealtimeThread and that such flexibility precludes the correct implementation of *any* known priority inversion algorithm when locked objects are accessed by instances of java.lang.Thread and NoHeapRealtimeThread, it is incumbent on the specification to provide alternate means for protected, concurrent data access by both types of threads (protected means access to data without the possibility of corruption). The three wait-free queue classes provide such access.

6.1   MonitorControl

Syntax: public abstract class MonitorControl

Direct Known Subclasses: PriorityCeilingEmulation$_{87}$, PriorityInheritance$_{88}$

Abstract superclass for all monitor control policy objects.

6.1.1   Constructors

public **MonitorControl**()

6.1.2   Methods

public static void **setMonitorControl**(MonitorControl$_{86}$ policy)
Control the default monitor behavior for object monitors used by
synchronized statements and methods in the system. The type of the policy
object determines the type of behavior. Conforming implementations must
support priority ceiling emulation and priority inheritance for fixed priority
preemptive threads.

Parameters:
> policy - The new monitor control policy. If null nothing happens.

public static void **setMonitorControl**(java.lang.Object monitor,
                MonitorControl$_{86}$ policy)
Has the same effect as setMonitorControl(), except that the policy only
affects the indicated object monitor.

Parameters:
> monitor - The monitor for which the new policy will be in use. The
> policy will take effect on the first attempt to lock the monitor
> after the completion of this method. If null nothing will happen.
> policy - The new policy for the object. If null nothing will happen.

6.2   PriorityCeilingEmulation

Syntax: public class PriorityCeilingEmulation extends MonitorControl$_{86}$

Monitor control class specifying use of the priority ceiling emulation protocol for
monitor objects. Objects under the influence of this protocol have the effect that a
thread entering the monitor has its effective priority — for priority-based dispatching
— raised to the ceiling on entry, and is restored to its previous effective priority when
it exits the monitor. See also MonitorControl$_{86}$ and PriorityInheritance$_{88}$.

6.2.1   Constructors

public **PriorityCeilingEmulation**(int ceiling)
Create a PriorityCeilingEmulation object with a given ceiling.

Parameters:
> ceiling - Priority ceiling value.

6.2.2   Methods

public int **getDefaultCeiling**()
> Get the priority ceiling for this PriorityCeilingEmulation object.

6.3   PriorityInheritance

Syntax: public class PriorityInheritance extends MonitorControl$_{86}$

Monitor control class specifying use of the priority inheritance protocol for object monitors. Objects under the influence of this protocol have the effect that a thread entering the monitor will boost the effective priority of the thread in the monitor to its own effective priority. When that thread exits the monitor, its effective priority will be restored to its previous value. See also MonitorControl$_{86}$ and PriorityCeilingEmulation$_{87}$

6.3.1   Constructors

public **PriorityInheritance**()

6.3.2   Methods

public static PriorityInheritance$_{88}$ **instance**()
> Return a pointer to the singleton PriorityInheritance.

6.4   WaitFreeDequeue

Syntax: public class WaitFreeDequeue

The wait-free queue classes facilitate communication and synchronization between instances of RealtimeThread$_{22}$ and java.lang.Thread . See WaitFreeWriteQueue$_{92}$ or WaitFreeReadQueue$_{90}$ for more details. Instances of this class create a WaitFreeWriteQueue$_{92}$ and a WaitFreeReadQueue$_{90}$ and make calls on the respective read() and write() methods.

6.4.1   Constructors

public **WaitFreeDequeue**(java.lang.Thread writer,
                          java.lang.Thread reader, intmaximum,
                          MemoryArea$_{60}$ area)
> A queue with unsynchronized and nonblocking read() and write() methods and synchronized and blocking read()and write() methods.

Parameters:

> `writer` - An instance of Thread.
>
> `reader` - An instance of Thread.
>
> `maximum` - Then maximum number of elements in the both the WaitFreeReadQueue$_{90}$ and the WaitFreeWriteQueue$_{92}$.
>
> `area` - The MemoryArea$_{60}$ in which this object and internal elements are allocated.

Throws: `InstantiationException`, `ClassNotFoundException`, `IllegalAccessException`, `IllegalArgumentException`

6.4.2 Methods

`public java.lang.Object` **`blockingRead`**`()`

A synchronized call of the `read()` method of the underlying WaitFreeWriteQueue$_{92}$. This call blocks on queue empty and will wait until there is an element in the queue to return.

Returns: An `java.lang.Object` from this.

`public boolean` **`blockingWrite`**`(java.lang.Object object)`

A synchronized call of the `write()` method of the underlying WaitFreeReadQueue$_{90}$. This call blocks on queue full and waits until there is space in this.

Parameters:

> `object` - The `java.lang.Object` to place in this.

Returns: True if `object` is now in this.

Throws: `MemoryScopeException`$_{155}$

`public boolean` **`force`**`(java.lang.Object object)`

If this is full then this call overwrites the last object written to this with the given object. If this is not full this call is equivalent to the `nonBlockingWrite()` call.

Parameters:

> `object` - The `java.lang.Object` which will overwrite the last object if this is full. Otherwise `object` will be placed in this.

`public java.lang.Object` **`nonBlockingRead`**`()`

An unsynchronized call of the `read()` method of the underlying WaitFreeReadQueue$_{90}$.

Returns: A `java.lang.Object` object read from this. If there are no elements in this then null is returned.

```
public boolean nonBlockingWrite(java.lang.Object object)
```
An unsynchronized call of the `write()` method of the underlying
WaitFreeWriteQueue$_{92}$. This call does not block on queue full.

Parameters:
> `object` - The `java.lang.Object` to attempt to place in this.

Returns: True if the `object` is now in this, otherwise returns false.

Throws: MemoryScopeException$_{155}$

6.5   WaitFreeReadQueue

Syntax: `public class WaitFreeReadQueue`

The wait-free queue classes facilitate communication and synchronization
between instances of RealtimeThread$_{22}$ and `java.lang.Thread`. The problem is
that synchronized access objects shared between real-time threads and threads might
cause the real-time threads to incur delays due to execution of the garbage collector.

The `read()` method of this class does not block on an imagined queue-empty
condition variable. If the `read()` is called on an empty queue null is returned. If two
real-time threads intend to read from this queue they must provide their own
synchronization.

The write method of this queue is synchronized and may be called by more than
one writer and will block on queue empty.

6.5.1   Constructors

```
public WaitFreeReadQueue(java.lang.Thread writer,
                java.lang.Thread reader, intmaximum,
                MemoryArea₆₀ memory)
```
A queue with an unsynchronized and nonblocking `read()` method and a
synchronized and blocking `write()` method. The memory areas of the
given threads are found. If these memory areas are the same the queue is
created in that memory area. If these memory areas are different the queue
is created in the memory area accessible by the most restricted thread type.

Parameters:
> `writer` - An instance of `java.lang.Thread`.
> `reader` - An instance of `java.lang.Thread`.
> `maximum` - The maximum number of elements in the queue.
> `memory` - The MemoryArea$_{60}$ in which this object and internal
> elements are stored.

Throws: IllegalAccessException, ClassNotFoundException,
InstantiationException, IllegalArgumentException

public **WaitFreeReadQueue**(java.lang.Thread writer,
java.lang.Thread reader, intmaximum,
MemoryArea$_{60}$ memory, boolean notify)

A queue with an unsynchronized and nonblocking read() method and a synchronized and blocking write() method.

Parameters:
writer - An instance of java.lang.Thread .
reader - An instance of java.lang.Thread .
maximum - The maximum number of elements in the queue.
memory - The MemoryArea$_{60}$ in which this object and internal elements are stored.
notify - Whether or not the reader is notified when data is added.

Throws: IllegalAccessException, ClassNotFoundException,
InstantiationException, IllegalArgumentException

6.5.2   Methods

public void **clear**()
Set this to empty.

public boolean **isEmpty**()
Used to determine if this is empty.

Returns: True if this is empty and false if this is not empty.

public boolean **isFull**()
Used to determine if this is full.

Returns: True if this is full and false if this is not full.

public java.lang.Object **read**()
Returns the next element in the queue unless the queue is empty. If the queue is empty null is returned.

public int **size**()
Used to determine the number of elements in this.

Returns: An integer which is the number of empty positions in this.

public void **waitForData**()
If this is empty waitForData() waits on the event until the writer inserts data. Note that true priority inversion does not occur since the writer locks a different object and the notify is executed by the AsyncEventHandler$_{127}$ which has noHeap characteristics.

```
public synchronized boolean write(java.lang.Object object)
```
The synchronized and blocking write. This call blocks on queue full and will wait until there is space in the queue.

Parameters:

> object - The java.lang.Object that is placed in this.

Throws: MemoryScopeException$_{155}$

6.6   WaitFreeWriteQueue

Syntax: public class WaitFreeWriteQueue

The wait-free queue classes facilitate communication and synchronization between instances of RealtimeThread$_{22}$ and java.lang.Thread . The problem is that synchronized access objects shared between real-time threads and threads might cause the real-time threads to incur delays due to execution of the garbage collector.

The write method of this class does not block on an imagined queue-full condition variable. If the write() method is called on a full queue false is returned. If two real-time threads intend to read from this queue they must provide their own synchronization.

The read() method of this queue is synchronized and may be called by more than one writer and will block on queue empty.

6.6.1   Constructors

```
public WaitFreeWriteQueue(java.lang.Thread writer,
                java.lang.Thread reader, intmaximum,
                MemoryArea60 memory)
```
A queue with an unsynchronized and nonblocking write() method and a synchronized and blocking read() method.

Parameters:

> writer - An instance of java.lang.Thread .
> reader - An instance of java.lang.Thread .
> maximum - The maximum number of elements in the queue.
> memory - The MemoryArea$_{60}$ in which this object and internal elements are allocated.

Throws: InstantiationException, ClassNotFoundException, IllegalAccessException, IllegalArgumentException

6.6.2 Methods

public void **bind**(java.lang.Thread writer, java.lang.Thread reader,
                    MemoryArea$_{60}$ memory)

Binds two threads together for the purpose of using this in each thread. If two unrelated (by common fixed memory area) threads are bound together, only immortal objects can be placed in the queue.

Parameters:

writer - The java.lang.Thread object which will write to this.
reader - The java.lang.Thread object which will read from this.
memory - The new MemoryArea$_{60}$ to use to test against the memory area of objects placed into this.

Throws: InstantiationException, IllegalAccessException, IllegalArgumentException

public void **clear**()
Set this to empty.

public boolean **force**(java.lang.Object object)
Force this java.lang.Object to replace the last one. If the reader should happen to have just removed the other java.lang.Object just as we were updating it, we will return false. False may mean that it just saw what we put in there. Either way, the best thing to do is to just write again — which will succeed, and check on the readers side for consecutive identical read values.

public boolean **isEmpty**()
Used to determine if this is empty.

Returns: True if this is empty and false if this is not empty.

public boolean **isFull**()
Used to determine if this is full.

Returns: True if this is full and false if this is not full.

public synchronized java.lang.Object **read**()
A synchronized read on the queue.

Returns: The java.lang.Object read or null if this is empty.

public int **size**()
Used to determine the number of elements in this.

Returns: An integer which is the number of empty positions in this.

public boolean **write**(java.lang.Object object)
Try to insert an element into the queue.

Parameters:
object - The java.lang.Object to insert.

Returns: True if the insert succeeded, false if not.

Throws: MemoryScopeException$_{155}$

Time

This section contains classes that:

- Allow description of a point in time with up to nanosecond accuracy and precision (actual accuracy and precision is dependent on the precision of the underlying system).
- Allow distinctions between absolute points in time, times relative to some starting point, and a new construct, rational time, which allows the efficient expression of occurrences per some interval of relative time.

The time classes required by the specification are `HighResolutionTime`, `AbsoluteTime`, `RelativeTime`, and `RationalTime`.

Instances of `HighResolutionTime` are not created, as the class exists to provide an implementation of the other three classes. An instance of `AbsoluteTime` encapsulates an absolute time expressed relative to midnight January 1, 1970 GMT. An instance of `RelativeTime` encapsulates a point in time that is relative to some other time value. Instances of `RationalTime` express a frequency by a numerator of type `long` (the frequency) and a denominator of type `RelativeTime`. If instances of `RationalTime` are given to certain constructors or methods the activity occurs for frequency times every interval. For example, if a `PeriodicTimer` is given an instance of `RationalTime` of (29,232) then the system will guarantee that the timer will fire exactly 29 times every 232 milliseconds even if the system has to slightly adjust the time between firings.

Semantics and Requirements

This list establishes the semantics and requirements that are applicable across the classes of this section. Semantics that apply to particular classes, constructors, methods, and fields will be found in the class description and the constructor, method, and field detail sections.

1. All time objects must maintain nanosecond precision and report their values in terms of millisecond and nanosecond constituents.
2. Time objects must be constructed from other time objects, or from millisecond/ nanosecond values.
3. Time objects must provide simple addition and subtraction operations, both for the entire object and for constituent parts.
4. Time objects must implement the `Comparable` interface if it is available. The `compareTo()` method must be implemented even if the interface is not available.
5. Any method of constructor that accepts a `RationalTime` of (x,y) must guarantee that its activity occurs exactly x times in every y milliseconds even if the intervals between occurrences of the activity have to be adjusted slightly. The RTSJ does not impose any required distribution on the lengths of the intervals but strongly suggests that implementations attempt to make them of approximately equal lengths.

Rationale

Time is the essence of real-time systems, and a method of expressing absolute time with sub-millisecond precision is an absolute minimum requirement. Expressing time in terms of nanoseconds has precedent and allows the implementation to provide time-based services, such as timers, using whatever precision it is capable of while the application requirements are expressed to an arbitrary level of precision.

The expression of millisecond and nanosecond constituents is consistent with other Java interfaces.

The expression of relative times allows for time-based metaphors such as deadline-based periodic scheduling where the cost of the task is expressed as a relative time and deadlines are usually represented as times relative to the beginning of the period.

7.1   HighResolutionTime

Syntax: `public abstract class HighResolutionTime implements`
`    java.lang.Comparable`

Direct Known Subclasses: AbsoluteTime_{99}, $\text{RelativeTime}_{102}$

All Implemented Interfaces: java.lang.Comparable

Used to express time with nanosecond accuracy. This class is never used directly: it is abstract and has no public constructors. Instead, use one of its subclasses AbsoluteTime_{99}, $\text{RelativeTime}_{102}$, or $\text{RationalTime}_{105}$. When an API is defined that has an `HighResolutionTime` as a parameter, it can take either an absolute, relative, or rational time and will do something appropriate. All of the arithmetic functions come in both allocating and non-allocating forms.

The standard Java `java.util.Date` class uses milliseconds as its basic unit in order to provide sufficient range for a wide variety of applications. Real-time programming generally requires nanosecond resolution, but even a 64 bit real-time clock based in nanoseconds would be problematic in some situations, so a compound format composed of 64 bits of millisecond timing, and 32 bits of nanoseconds within a millisecond, was chosen.

Caution: This class is explicitly unsafe in multithreaded situations when it is being changed. No synchronization is done. It is assumed that users of this class who are mutating instances will be doing their own synchronization at a higher level.

7.1.1   Methods

public abstract AbsoluteTime_{99} **absolute**(Clock_{110} clock,
                    AbsoluteTime_{99} dest)
Convert this time to an absolute time, relative to some clock. Convenient for situations where you really need an absolute time, but would like to allow relative times to be used too. Allocates a destination object if necessary. See the derived class comments for more specific information.

Parameters:
    clock - The Clock_{110} reference for relative times.
    dest - If null, a new object may or may not need to be allocated for the result.

Returns: AbsoluteTime_{99} version of this object.

public int **compareTo**($\text{HighResolutionTime}_{97}$ time)

> Compare this HighResolutionTime with the specified
> HighResolutionTime. This method is provided in preference to individual
> methods for each of the six boolean comparison operators (<, ==, >, >=, !=,
> <=). The suggested idiom for performing these comparisons is:
> (x.compareTo(y) <op> 0), where <op> is one of the six comparison
> operators.

public int **compareTo**(java.lang.Object object)
> For the Comparable interface.

public boolean **equals**(HighResolutionTime$_{97}$ time)
> Return true if the argument object has the same values as this.

> *Parameters:*
>> time - Values are compared to this.

public boolean **equals**(java.lang.Object object)
> Return true if the argument is a HighResolutionTime reference and has the
> same values as this.

> *Overrides:* java.lang.Object.equals(java.lang.Object) in class
>> java.lang.Object

> *Parameters:*
>> object - Values are compared to this.

public final long **getMilliseconds**()
> Return the milliseconds component of this.

> *Returns:* The milliseconds component of the time past the epoch
>> represented by this.

public final int **getNanoseconds**()
> Return nanoseconds component of this.

> *Returns:* The nanoseconds component of the time past the epoch
>> represented by this.

public int **hashCode**()

> *Overrides:* java.lang.Object.hashCode() in class java.lang.Object

public void **set**(HighResolutionTime$_{97}$ time)
> Changes the time represented by the argument to some time between the
> invocation of the method and the return of the method.

> *Parameters:*
>> time - The HighResolutionTime which will be set to represent the
>>> current time.

```
public void set(long millis)
```
Set the millisecond component of this to the given argument.

Parameters:
> millis - This value will be the value of the millisecond component of this at the completion of the call. If millis is negative the millisecond value of this is set to the negative value. Although logically this may represent time before the epoch, invalid results may occur if a HighResolutionTime representing time before the epoch is given as a parameter to other methods.

```
public void set(long millis, intnanos)
```
Set the millisecond and nanosecond components of this to the given arguments. If millis plus nanos result in a negative value the time represented by this is time before the epoch. Although reasonable invalid results may occur if a HighResolutionTime representing time before the epoch is given as a parameter to other methods.

Parameters:
> millis - This value will be the value of the millisecond component of this at the completion of the call.
> nanos - This value will be the value of the nanosecond component of this at the completion of the call.

7.2   AbsoluteTime

Syntax: public class AbsoluteTime extends HighResolutionTime$_{97}$

All Implemented Interfaces: java.lang.Comparable

An object that represents a specific point in time given by milliseconds plus nanoseconds past the epoch (January 1, 1970, 00:00:00 GMT). This representation was designed to be compatible with the standard Java representation of an absolute time in the java.util.Date class.

Caution: This class is explicitly unsafe in multithreaded situations when it is being changed. No synchronization is done. It is assumed that users of this class who are mutating instances will be doing their own synchronization at a higher level.

7.2.1   Constructors

```
public AbsoluteTime()
```
Equivalent to new AbsoluteTime(0,0)

```
public AbsoluteTime(AbsoluteTime99 time)
```

Make a new AbsoluteTime$_{99}$ object from the given AbsoluteTime$_{99}$ object.

Parameters:
> time - The AbsoluteTime$_{99}$ object used as the source for the copy.

public **AbsoluteTime**(java.util.Date date)
Equivalent to new AbsoluteTime(date.getTime(),0).

Parameters:
> date - The java.util.Date representation of time past the epoch.

public **AbsoluteTime**(long millis, int nanos)
Constructs an AbsoluteTime$_{99}$ object, which means a time millis milliseconds plus nanos nanoseconds past 00:00:00 GMT on January 1, 1970. If the addition of millis and nanos results in a negative value, although reasonable in that it represents a time before the epoch, then invalid output may occur when this is used as an argument to other methods.

Parameters:
> millis - The milliseconds component of the time past the epoch.
> nanos - The nanosecond component of the time past the epoch.

7.2.2   Methods

public AbsoluteTime$_{99}$ **absolute**(Clock$_{110}$ clock,
                    AbsoluteTime$_{99}$ destination)
Convert this time to an absolute time. For an AbsoluteTime$_{99}$, this is real easy: it just returns itself. Presume that this time is already relative to the given clock.

Overrides: public abstract AbsoluteTime99 absolute(Clock110
> clock, AbsoluteTime99 dest)$_{97}$ in class
> HighResolutionTime$_{97}$

Parameters:
> clock - Clock$_{110}$ on which this is based.
> destination - Converted to an absolute time.

public AbsoluteTime$_{99}$ **add**(long millis, intnanos)
A new object is allocated for the result.

Parameters:
> millis - Values are added to this.
> nanos - Rest of value added to this.

```
public AbsoluteTime99 add(long millis, intnanos,
                AbsoluteTime99 destination)
```
If destination is non-null, the result is placed there and destination is returned. Otherwise a new object is allocated for the result.

Parameters:

> millis - Value is added to this.
> nanos - Rest of value added to this.
> destination - Result is placed here if non-null.

Returns: An AbsoluteTime99. A result is always returned. A new object is created if destination is null.

```
public final AbsoluteTime99 add(RelativeTime102 time)
```
Return this+b. A new object is allocated for the result.

Parameters:

> time - Values are added to this.

```
public AbsoluteTime99 add(RelativeTime102 time,
                AbsoluteTime99 destination)
```
Return this+time. If dest is non-null, the result is placed there and dest is returned. Otherwise a new object is allocated for the result.

Parameters:

> time - Values are added to this.
> destination - Result is placed here if non-null.

Returns: An AbsoluteTime99. A result is always returned. A new object is created if dest is null.

```
public java.util.Date getDate()
```
Return the time past the epoch represented by this as a java.util.Date.

```
public void set(java.util.Date date)
```
Change the time represented by this.

Parameters:

> date - java.util.Date which becomes the time represented by this after the completion of this method.

```
public final RelativeTime102 subtract(AbsoluteTime99 time)
```
Return this-time. A new object is allocated for the result.

Parameters:

> time - Values are added to this.

```
public RelativeTime102 subtract(AbsoluteTime99 time,
                RelativeTime102 destination)
```

Return this-time. If destination is non-null, the result is placed there and destination is returned. Otherwise a new object is allocated for the result

Parameters:
> time - Values are subtracted from this.
> destination - Result is placed here if non-null.

Returns: An AbsoluteTime$_{99}$. A result is always returned. A new object is created if destination is null.

public final AbsoluteTime$_{99}$ **subtract**(RelativeTime$_{102}$ time)
Return this-time. A new object is allocated for the result.

Parameters:
> time - Values are added to this.

public AbsoluteTime$_{99}$ **subtract**(RelativeTime$_{102}$ time,
                AbsoluteTime$_{99}$ destination)
Return this-time. If destination is non-null, the result is placed there and destination is returned. Otherwise a new object is allocated for the result.

Parameters:
> time - Values are subtracted from this.
> destination - Result is placed here if non-null.

Returns: An AbsoluteTime$_{99}$. A result is always returned. A new object is created if destination is null.

public java.lang.String **toString**()
Return a printable version of this Time, in a format that matches java.util.Date.toString() with a postfix to detail the sub-second value.

Overrides: java.lang.Object.toString() in class java.lang.Object

---

7.3   RelativeTime

Syntax: public class RelativeTime extends HighResolutionTime$_{97}$

Direct Known Subclasses: RationalTime$_{105}$

All Implemented Interfaces: java.lang.Comparable

An object that represents a time interval millis/1E3+nanos/1E9 seconds long. It generally is used to represent a time relative to *now*.

Caution: This class is explicitly unsafe in multithreaded situations when it is being changed. No synchronization is done. It is assumed that users of this class who are mutating instances will be doing their own synchronization at a higher level.

7.3.1   Constructors

public **RelativeTime**()
> Equivalent to new RelativeTime(0,0).

public **RelativeTime**(long millis, int nanos)
> Construct a new RelativeTime object from the given millisecond and nanosecond components.

public **RelativeTime**(RelativeTime$_{102}$ time)
> Construct a new RelativeTime object from the given RelativeTime.

7.3.2   Methods

public AbsoluteTime$_{99}$ **absolute**(Clock$_{110}$ clock,
> AbsoluteTime$_{99}$ destination)

> Convert this time to an absolute time. For a RelativeTime, this involves adding the clock's conception of now to this interval and constructing a new AbsoluteTime$_{99}$ based on the sum.

> *Overrides:* public abstract AbsoluteTime99 absolute(Clock110 clock, AbsoluteTime99 dest)$_{97}$ in class HighResolutionTime$_{97}$

> *Parameters:*
>> clock - If null Clock.getRealtimeClock() is used.
>> destination - If null it is set to c.getTime() otherwise c.getTime(dest) is called.

public RelativeTime$_{102}$ **add**(long millis, int nanos)
> A new object is allocated for the result.

> *Parameters:*
>> millis - Values are added to this.
>> nanos - Rest of value added to this.

public RelativeTime$_{102}$ **add**(long millis, int nanos,
> RelativeTime$_{102}$ destination)

> If destination is non-null, the result is placed there and destination is returned. Otherwise a new object is allocated for the result.

Parameters:
> `millis` - Value is added to this.
> `nanos` - Rest of value added to this.
> `destination` - Result is placed here if non-null.

Returns: A `RelativeTime`. A result is always returned. A new object is created if `destination` is null.

`public final RelativeTime`$_{102}$ **`add`**`(RelativeTime`$_{102}$ `time)`
Return `this+time`. A new object is allocated for the result.

Parameters:
> `time` - Values are added to this.

`public RelativeTime`$_{102}$ **`add`**`(RelativeTime`$_{102}$ `time,`
            `RelativeTime`$_{102}$ `destination)`
Return `this+time`. If `destination` is non-null, the result is placed there and `destination` is returned. Otherwise a new object is allocated for the result.

Parameters:
> `time` - Values are added to this.
> `destination` - Result is placed here if non-null.

Returns: A `RelativeTime`. A Result is always returned. A new object is created if `destination` is null.

`public void` **`addInterarrivalTo`**`(AbsoluteTime`$_{99}$ `destination)`
Add this time to an `AbsoluteTime`$_{99}$. It is almost the same as `destination.add(this,dest)` except that it accounts for (i.e., divides by) the frequency.

`public RelativeTime`$_{102}$ **`getInterarrivalTime`**`(RelativeTime`$_{102}$
            `destination)`
Return the interarrival time that is the result of dividing this interval by its frequency. For a `RelativeTime`, and `RationalTime`$_{105}$ s with a frequency of 1, it just returns this. The interarrival time is necessarily an approximation.

`public final RelativeTime`$_{102}$ **`subtract`**`(RelativeTime`$_{102}$ `time)`
Return `this-time`. A new object is allocated for the result.

Parameters:
> `time` - Values are added to this.

`public RelativeTime`$_{102}$ **`subtract`**`(RelativeTime`$_{102}$ `time,`
            `RelativeTime`$_{102}$ `destination)`

Return `this-time`. If `destination` is non-null, the result is placed there and `destination` is returned. Otherwise a new object is allocated for the result.

Parameters:
> `time` - Values are subtracted from this.
> `destination` - Result is placed here if non-null.

Returns: A `RelativeTime`. A result is always returned. A new object is created if `destination` is null.

public java.lang.String **toString**()
> Return a printable version of this time.

> *Overrides:* java.lang.Object.toString() in class java.lang.Object

7.4 RationalTime

Syntax: `public class RationalTime extends RelativeTime`$_{102}$

All Implemented Interfaces: java.lang.Comparable

An object that represents a time interval millis/1E3+nanos/1E9 seconds long that is divided into subintervals by some frequency. This is generally used in periodic events, threads, and feasibility analysis to specify periods where there is a basic period that must be adhered to strictly (the interval), but within that interval the periodic events are supposed to happen *frequency* times, as uniformly spaced as possible, but clock and scheduling jitter is moderately acceptable.

Caution: This class is explicitly unsafe in multithreaded situations when it is being changed. No synchronization is done. It is assumed that users of this class who are mutating instances will be doing their own synchronization at a higher level.

7.4.1 Constructors

public **RationalTime**(int frequency)
> Equivalent to new `RationalTime(frequency,1000,0)` which represents a cycles-per-second value.

public **RationalTime**(int frequency, longmillis, intnanos)
> Create a `RationalTime` that indicates `frequency` occurrences of something (e.g. firings of a `PeriodicTimer`$_{114}$) in an interval of time millis/1E3+nanos/1E9 seconds long.

Parameters:

frequency - The number of occurrences indicated for the given
time.

millis - The millisecond component of the time interval.

nanos - The nanosecond component of the time interval.

Throws: IllegalArgumentException - Thrown if the frequence, millis,
or nanos value is less than zero, or if the computed time interval
is less than or equal to zero.

public **RationalTime**(int frequency, RelativeTime$_{102}$ interval)
Create a RationalTime that indicates frequency occurrences of something
(e.g. firings of a PeriodicTimer$_{114}$) in an interval of time.

Parameters:
frequency - The number of occurrences indicated for the given
interval.

interval - The interval expressed as a RelativeTime$_{102}$.

Throws: IllegalArgumentException - Thrown if the frequence is less
than zero.

7.4.2   Methods

public AbsoluteTime$_{99}$ **absolute**(Clock$_{110}$ clock,
AbsoluteTime$_{99}$ destination)
Convert this time to an absolute time, relative to some clock. Convenient
for situations where you really need an absolute time, but would like to
allow rational times to be used too. Allocates a destination object if
necessary. See the derived class comments for more specific information.

Overrides: public AbsoluteTime99 absolute(Clock110 clock,
AbsoluteTime99 destination)$_{103}$ in class RelativeTime$_{102}$

Parameters:
clock - The Clock$_{110}$ reference for relative times.

destination - If null, a new object may or may not need to be
allocated for the result.

Returns: An AbsoluteTime$_{99}$ version of this object.

public void **addInterarrivalTo**(AbsoluteTime$_{99}$ destination)
Add this time to an AbsoluteTime$_{99}$. It is almost the same as
destination.add(this,destination) except that it accounts for (i.e.,
divides by) the frequency.

Overrides: public void addInterarrivalTo(AbsoluteTime99
destination)$_{104}$ in class RelativeTime$_{102}$

```
public int getFrequency()
```
Return the frequency component of this.

```
public RelativeTime102 getInterarrivalTime(RelativeTime102 dest)
```
Return the interarrival time that is the result of dividing this interval by its frequency. For RationalTime instances with a frequency of 1, it just returns this. The interarrival time is necessarily an approximation (partly because of numerical imprecision and partly because of clock/scheduling jitter).

> *Overrides:* public RelativeTime102 getInterarrivalTime(RelativeTime102 destination)$_{104}$ in class RelativeTime$_{102}$

```
public void set(long millis, intnanos)
```
Change the indicated interval of this to the sum of the values of the arguments.

> *Overrides:* public void set(long millis, intnanos) $_{99}$ in class HighResolutionTime$_{97}$

> *Throws:* IllegalArgumentException - Thrown if the millis, or nanos value is less than zero, or if the computed time interval is less than or equal to zero.

```
public void setFrequency(int frequency)
```
Change the frequency of this to the given value.

> *Throws:* ArithmeticException - Thrown if the frequency is less than zero.

HighResolutionTime Example

HighResolutionTime defines the base class for AbsoluteTime and RelativeTime. You cannot create HighResolutionTime objects directly, you must use one of the subclasses:

```
AbsoluteTime at;
```

All high resolution times are a normal java time: a long(64 bit) time in milliseconds; plus an offset in nanoseconds. All constructors take the same (milliseconds, nanoseconds) parameters, along with some variants for convenience:

```
at = new AbsoluteTime(System.currentTimeMillis(), 0);
System.out.print("at=" + at + "\n");
```

Relative times refer to an interval and can be added to another time:

```
RelativeTime step = new RelativeTime(0, 500); //500nanosecond s
System.out.print("sum=" + at.add(step) + "\n");
```

Offset computations can be performed more simply with built in methods:

```
System.out.print("sum2=" + at.addNanoseconds(500) + "\n");
```

All of the math methods return their results as a `HighResolutionTime`. They all normally allocate a new object for their return value, but they all also have alternative forms that allow the destination to be specified:

```
AbsoluteTime dest = new AbsoluteTime(0, 0);
at.add(step, dest);
System.out.print("sum3=" + dest + "\n");
```

The destination can be the same as the object to which the method is applied. This allows for in-place modification of the time:

```
at.addNanoseconds(500, at);
System.out.print("sum4=" + at + "\n");
```

Output from running the example

```
at=Thu Mar 23 14:01:04 PST 2000+517ms
sum=Thu Mar 23 14:01:04 PST 2000+517000500ns
sum2=Thu Mar 23 14:01:04 PST 2000+517001000ns
sum3=Thu Mar 23 14:01:04 PST 2000+517000500ns
sum4=Thu Mar 23 14:01:04 PST 2000+517001000ns
```

CHAPTER **8**

Timers

This section contains classes that:

- Allow creation of a timer whose expiration is either periodic or set to occur at a particular time as kept by a system-dependent time base (clock).
- Trigger some behavior to occur on expiration of a timer, using the asynchronous event mechanisms provided by the specification.

The classes provided by this section are `Clock`, `Timer`, `PeriodicTimer`, and `OneShotTimer`.

An instance of the `Clock` class is provided by the implementation. There is normally one clock provided, the system real-time clock. This object provides the mechanism for triggering behavior on expiration of a timer. It also reports the resolution of timers provided by the implementation.

An instance of `PeriodicTimer` fires an AsyncEvent at constant intervals.

An instance of `OneShotTimer` describes an event that is to be triggered exactly once at either an absolute time, or at a time relative to the creation of the timer. It may be used as the source for timeouts.

Instances of `Timer` are not used. The `Timer` class provides the interface and underlying implementation for both one-shot and periodic timers.

Semantics and Requirements

This list establishes the semantics and requirements that are applicable across the classes of this section. Semantics that apply to particular classes, constructors,

109

methods, and fields will be found in the class description and the constructor, method, and field detail sections.

1. The Clock class shall be capable of reporting the achievable resolution of timers based on that clock.
2. The OneShotTimer class shall ensure that a one-shot timer is triggered exactly once, regardless of whether or not the timer is enabled after expiration of the indicated time.
3. The PeriodicTimer class shall allow the period of the timer to be expressed in terms of a RelativeTime or a RationalTime. In the latter case, the implementation shall provide a best effort to perform any correction necessary to maintain the frequency at which the event occurs.
4. If a periodic timer is enabled after expiration of the start time, the first event shall occur immediately and thus mark the start of the first period.

Rationale

The importance of the use of one-shot timers for timeout behavior and the vagaries in the execution of code prior to enabling the timer for short timeouts dictate that the triggering of the timer should be guaranteed. The problem is exacerbated for periodic timers where the importance of the periodic triggering outweighs the precision of the start time. In such cases, it is also convenient to allow, for example, a relative time of zero to be used as the start time for relative timers.

In many situations, it is important that a periodic task be represented as a frequency and that the period remain synchronized. In these cases, a relatively simple correction can be enforced by the implementation at the expense of some additional overhead for the timer.

8.1   Clock

Syntax: public abstract class Clock

A clock advances from the past, through the present, into the future. It has a concept of *now* that can be queried through Clock.getTime(), and it can have events queued on it which will be fired when their appointed time is reached. There are many possible subclasses of clocks: real-time clocks, user time clocks, simulation time clocks. The idea of using multiple clocks may at first seem unusual but we allow it as a possible resource allocation strategy.

Consider a real-time system where the natural events of the system have different tolerances for jitter (jitter refers to the distribution of the differences between when the events are actually raised or noticed by the software and when they should have really occurred according to time in the real-world). Assume the system functions properly if event *A* is noticed or raised within plus or minus 100 seconds of the actual time it should occur but event *B* must be noticed or raised within 100 microseconds of its actual time. Further assume, without loss of generality, that events *A* and *B* are periodic. An application could then create two instances of PeriodicTimer$_{114}$ based on two clocks. The timer for event *B* should be based on a Clock which checks its queue at least every 100 microseconds but the timer for event *A* could be based on a Clock that checked its queue only every 100 seconds. This use of two clocks reduces the queue size of the accurate clock and thus queue management overhead is reduced.

8.1.1 Constructors

public **Clock**()

8.1.2 Methods

public static Clock$_{110}$ **getRealtimeClock**()
> There is always one clock object available: a real-time clock that advances in sync with the external world. This is the default Clock.

> *Returns:* An instance of the default Clock.

public abstract RelativeTime$_{102}$ **getResolution**()
> Return the resolution of the clock, that is, the interval between ticks. Note that neither a clock or any software using this clock can know about events that occur between ticks. In some sense all events happen in the past and we only care if the past gets too long.

> *Returns:* A RelativeTime$_{102}$ object representing the resolution of this.

public AbsoluteTime$_{99}$ **getTime**()
> Return the current time in a freshly allocated object.

> *Returns:* An AbsoluteTime$_{99}$ that represents the current time of this.

public abstract void **getTime**(AbsoluteTime$_{99}$ time)
> Return the current time in an existing object. The time represented by the given AbsoluteTime$_{99}$ is changed some time between the invocation of the method and the return of the method.

> *Parameters:*
>> time - The AbsoluteTime$_{99}$ object which will have its time changed. If null then nothing happens.

public abstract void **setResolution**(RelativeTime$_{102}$ resolution)
> Sets the resolution of this. However, some hardware clocks do not allow changes in resolution. If this method is called on one those the method will complete but the resolution will not change.

Parameters:
> resolution - The new resolution of this.

8.2   Timer

Syntax: public abstract class Timer extends AsyncEvent$_{125}$

Direct Known Subclasses: OneShotTimer$_{113}$, PeriodicTimer$_{114}$

A Timer is a timed event that measures time relative to a given Clock$_{110}$. This class defines basic functionality available to all timers. Applications will generally use either PeriodicTimer$_{114}$ to create an event that is fired repeatedly at regular intervals, or OneShotTimer$_{113}$ for an event that just fires once at a specific time. A timer is always based on a Clock$_{110}$, which provides the basic facilities of something that ticks along following some time line (real-time, cpu-time, user-time, simulation-time, etc.). All timers are created disabled and do nothing until start() is called.

8.2.1   Constructors

protected **Timer**(HighResolutionTime$_{97}$ t, Clock$_{110}$ c,
              AsyncEventHandler$_{127}$ handler)
> Create a Timer.

Parameters:
> t - The time to fire the event. Will be converted to absolute time.
> c - The Clock$_{110}$ on which to base this time. If null, the system real-time clock is used.
> handler - The default handler to use for this event. If null, no handler is associated with it and nothing will happen when this event fires until a handler is provided.

8.2.2   Methods

public ReleaseParameters$_{43}$ **createReleaseParameters**()

> *Overrides:* public ReleaseParameters43
>   createReleaseParameters()$_{126}$ in class AsyncEvent$_{125}$

public void **disable**()
>   Disable this timer, preventing it from firing. It may subsequently be re-enabled. If the timer is disabled when its fire time occurs, then it will not fire. However, a disabled timer continues to count while it is disabled, and if it is subsequently re-enabled before its fire time occurs and is enabled when its fire time occurs it will fire then. If it is enabled after its fire time has occurred then it will fire immediately.

public void **enable**()
>   Re-enable this timer after it has been disabled.

public Clock$_{110}$ **getClock**()
>   Used to determine the clock with which this is associated and is thus used to decrement the implicit counter for this.
>
>   *Returns:* A Clock$_{110}$ object which is the clock associated with this.

public AbsoluteTime$_{99}$ **getFireTime**()
>   Get the time at which this event will fire. The value returned is not dependent on whether or not this is enabled or disabled.
>
>   *Returns:* An AbsoluteTime$_{99}$ object representing the absolute time at which this will fire.

public void **reschedule**(HighResolutionTime$_{97}$ time)
>   Change the scheduled time for this event. Can take either absolute or relative times.
>
>   *Parameters:*
>>   time - The new time at which this will fire. If null the previous fire time is still the time at which this will fire.

public void **start**()
>   A Timer starts measuring time from when it is started.

8.3   OneShotTimer

Syntax: public class OneShotTimer extends Timer$_{112}$

A timed AsyncEvent$_{125}$ that is driven by a clock. It will fire off once, when the clock time reaches the timeout time. If clock time has already passed the timeout time, it will fire immediately.

8.3.1   Constructors

public **OneShotTimer**(HighResolutionTime$_{97}$ time,
                 AsyncEventHandler$_{127}$ handler)

Create an instance of AsyncEvent$_{125}$ that will execute its fire method at the expiration of the given time.

Parameters:
> time - Will fire at time.absolute(). Null equals *now.*
> handler - The AsyncEventHandler$_{127}$ that will be scheduled when AsyncEvent.fire() is executed.

public **OneShotTimer**(HighResolutionTime$_{97}$ start, Clock$_{110}$ clock,
                      AsyncEventHandler$_{127}$ handler)
Create an instance of AsyncEvent$_{125}$, based on the given clock, that will execute its fire method at the expiration of the given time.

Parameters:
> start - Will fire at start.absolute(). Null equals *now.*
> clock - The timer will increment based on this clock.
> handler - The AsyncEventHandler$_{127}$ that will be scheduled when AsyncEvent.fire() is executed.

8.4   PeriodicTimer

Syntax: public class PeriodicTimer extends Timer$_{112}$

An AsyncEvent$_{125}$ whose fire method is executed periodically according to the given parameters. If a clock is given, calculation of the period uses the increments of the clock. If an interval is given or set the system guarantees that the fire method will execute interval time units after the last execution or its given start time as appropriate. If one of the HighResolutionTime$_{97}$ argument types is RationalTime$_{105}$ then the system guarantees that the fire method will be executed exactly frequency times every unit time (see RationalTime$_{105}$ constructors) by adjusting the interval between executions of fire().

This is similar to a thread with PeriodicParameters$_{45}$ except that it is lighter weight.

If a PeriodicTimer is disabled, it still counts, and if enabled at some later time, it will fire at its next scheduled fire time.

8.4.1   Constructors

public **PeriodicTimer**(HighResolutionTime$_{97}$ start,
                       RelativeTime$_{102}$ interval,
                       AsyncEventHandler$_{127}$ handler)
Create an instance of AsyncEvent$_{125}$ that executes its fire() method periodically.

Parameters:

> start - When the first interval begins. Null equals *now*.
>
> interval - The time between successive executions of the fire()
> method.
>
> handler - The instance of AsyncEventHandler$_{127}$ that will be
> scheduled each time the fire method is executed.

public **PeriodicTimer**(HighResolutionTime$_{97}$ start,
 RelativeTime$_{102}$ interval, Clock$_{110}$ clock,
 AsyncEventHandler$_{127}$ handler)

Create an instance of AsyncEvent$_{125}$ that executes its fire() method
periodically.

Parameters:

> start - When the first interval begins. Null equals *now*.
>
> interval - The time between successive executions of the fire()
> method.
>
> clock - The Clock$_{110}$ whose increments are used to calculate the
> interval.
>
> handler - The instance of AsyncEventHandler$_{127}$ that will be
> scheduled each time the fire method is executed.

8.4.2 Methods

public ReleaseParameters$_{43}$ **createReleaseParameters**()

Create a ReleaseParameters$_{43}$ object with the next fire time as the start
time and the interval of this as the period.

Overrides: public ReleaseParameters43
 createReleaseParameters()$_{112}$ in class Timer$_{112}$

public void **fire**()

The only real difference between a periodic timer and a one-shot timer is
that a periodic timer contiues to fire once each period.

Overrides: public synchronized void fire()$_{126}$ in class
 AsyncEvent$_{125}$

public AbsoluteTime$_{99}$ **getFireTime**()

Get the next time at which this will fire. The value returned is not
dependent on whether or not this is enabled or disabled.

Overrides: public AbsoluteTime99 getFireTime()$_{113}$ in class Timer$_{112}$

Returns: An AbsoluteTime$_{99}$ object representing the absolute time at
 which this will fire.

```
public RelativeTime_{102} getInterval()
     Return the interval of this Timer_{112}.
```

Returns: A RelativeTime$_{102}$ object which is the current interval of this.

```
public void setInterval(RelativeTime_{102} interval)
     Reset the interval of this Timer_{112}.
```

Timer Example

Here's a definition of the Scheduling parameters for a high priority task that we'll
create later:

```
SchedulingParameters highPriority =
   new PriorityParameters(PriorityScheduler.getMaxPriority());
```

This method is a generic testbed for showing what timers do:

```
private static void TestTimer(String title, Timer t)
{
   System.out.print("\n" + title + " test:\n");
```

Figure out the start time:

```
final long T0 = t.getFireTime().getMilliseconds();
```

Ask the timer to create the appropriate release parameters:

```
ReleaseParameters rp = t.createReleaseParameters();
```

Fill in a guess at the handlers runtime:

```
rp.setCost(new RelativeTime(10, 0)); / / agues satruntim e i n
System.out.print("  Release parameters=" + rp + "\n");
```

Add a handler that prints a message when the timer fires off:

```
t.addHandler(new AsyncEventHandler(highPriority, rp, null) {
   public void handleAsyncEvent() {
      System.out.print("  Timer went off at "
    + (System.currentTimeMillis() - T0) + "\n");
   }
});
```

Give the timer a kick:

```
t.start();
```

And wait a while to watch things happen:

```
try {
  Thread.sleep(1000);
} catch(InterruptedException ie) {
}
System.out.print("  After sleeping, t="
  + (System.currentTimeMillis() - T0) + "\n");
```

Run the test bed with a one shot timer:

```
TestTimer("One Shot",
  new OneShotTimer(new RelativeTime(100, 0), null));
```

Then with a periodic timer:

```
TestTimer("Periodic",
  new PeriodicTimer(new RelativeTime(100, 0),
    new RelativeTime(100, 0), null));
```

CHAPTER 9

Asynchrony

This section contains classes that:

- Provide mechanisms that bind the execution of program logic to the occurrence of internal and external events.
- Provide mechanisms that allow the asynchronous transfer of control.
- Provide mechanisms that allow the asynchronous termination of threads.

This specification provides several facilities for arranging asynchronous control of execution, some of which apply to threads in general while others apply only to real-time threads. These facilities fall into two main categories: asynchronous event handling and asynchronous transfer of control (ATC), which includes thread termination.

Asynchronous event handling is captured by the non-abstract class AsyncEvent and the abstract classes AsyncEventHandler and BoundAsyncEventHandler. An instance of the AsyncEvent class is an object corresponding to the possibility of an asynchronous event occurrence. An event occurrence may be initiated by either application logic or by the occurrence of a *happening* external to the JVM (such as a software signal or a hardware interrupt handler). An event occurrence is expressed in program logic by the invocation of the fire() method of an instance of the AsyncEvent class. The initiation of an event occurrence due to a happening is implementation dependent.

An instance of the class AsyncEventHandler is an object embodying code that is scheduled in response to the occurrence of an event. The run() method of an instance of AsyncEventHandler acts like a thread, and indeed one of its constructors takes references to instances of SchedulingParameters, ReleaseParameters, and

MemoryParameters. However, there is not necessarily a separate thread for each run() method. The class BoundAsyncEventHandler extends AsyncEventHandler, and should be used if it is necessary to ensure that a handler has a dedicated thread. An event count is maintained so that a handler can cope with event bursts — situations where an event is fired more frequently than its handler can respond.

The interrupt() method in java.lang.Thread provides rudimentary asynchronous communication by setting a pollable/resettable flag in the target thread, and by throwing a synchronous exception when the target thread is blocked at an invocation of wait(), sleep(), or join(). This specification extends the effect of Thread.interrupt() and adds an overloaded version in RealtimeThread, offering a more comprehensive and non-polling asynchronous execution control facility. It is based on throwing and propagating exceptions that, though asynchronous, are deferred where necessary in order to avoid data structure corruption. The main elements of ATC are embodied in the class AsynchronouslyInterruptedException (AIE), its subclass Timed, the interface Interruptible, and in the semantics of the interrupt methods in Thread and RealtimeThread.

A method indicates its willingness to be asynchronously interrupted by including AIE on its throws clause. If a thread is asynchronously interrupted while executing a method that identifies AIE on its throws clause, then an instance of AIE will be thrown as soon as the thread is outside of a section in whichATC is deferred. Several idioms are available for handling an AIE, giving the programmer the choice of using catch clauses and a low-level mechanism with specific control over propagation, or a higher-level facility that allows specifying the interruptible code, the handler, and the result retrieval as separate methods.

Semantics and Requirements

This list establishes the semantics and requirements that are applicable to AsyncEvent objects. Semantics that apply to particular classes, constructors, methods, and fields will be found in the class description and the constructor, method, and field detail sections.

1. When an instance of AsyncEvent occurs (by either program logic or a happening), all run() methods of instances of the AsyncEventHandler class that have been added to the instance of AsyncEvent by the execution of addHandler() are scheduled for execution. This action may or may not be idempotent. Every occurrence of an event increments a counter in each associated handler. Handlers may elect to execute logic for each occurrence of the event or not.

2. Instances of `AsyncEvent` and `AsyncEventHandler` may be created and used by any program logic.

3. More than one instance of `AsyncEventHandler` may be added to an instance of `AsyncEvent`.

4. An instance of `AsyncEventHandler` may be added to more than one instance of `AsyncEvent`.

This list establishes the semantics and requirements that are applicable to `AsynchronouslyInterruptedException`. Semantics that apply to particular classes, constructors, methods, and fields will be found in the class description and the constructor, method, and field detail sections.

1. Instances of the class `AsynchronouslyInterruptedException` can be generated by execution of program logic and by internal virtual machine mechanisms that are asynchronous to the execution of program logic which is the target of the exception.

2. Program logic that exists in methods that throw `AsynchronouslyInterruptedException` is subject to receiving an instance of `AsynchronouslyInterruptedException` at any time during execution.

3. The RTSJ specifically requires that blocking methods in `java.io.*` must be prevented from blocking indefinitely when invoked from a method with AIE in its `throws` clause. The implementation, when either `AIE.fire()` or `RealtimeThread.interrupt()` is called when control is in a `java.io.*` method invoked from an interruptible method, may either unblock the blocked call, raise an `IOException` on behalf of the call, or allow the call to complete normally if the implementation determines that the call would eventually unblock.

4. Program logic executing within a `synchronized` block within a method with `AsynchronouslyInterruptedException` in its `throws` clause is not subject to receiving an instance of AIE. The interrupted state of the execution context is set to pending and the program logic will receive the instance when control passes out of the `synchronized` block if other semantics in this list so indicate.

5. Constructors are allowed to include `AsynchronouslyInterruptedException` in their `throws` clause and will thus be interruptible.

Definitions

The RTSJ's approach to ATC is designed to follow these principles. It is based on exceptions and is an extension of the current Java language rules for `java.lang.Thread.interrupt()`. The following terms and abbreviations will be used:

ATC - Asynchronous Transfer of Control

AIE - (Asynchronously Interrupted Exception) The class
`javax.realtime.AsynchronouslyInterruptedException`, a subclass of
`java.lang.InterruptedException`.

AI - (Asynchronously Interruptible) A method is said to be asynchronously
interruptible if it includes AIE in its throws clause.

ATC-deferred section - a synchronized method, a synchronized statement, or any
method or constructor without AIE in its throws clause.

Summary of Operation

In summary, ATC works as follows:

If `t` is an instance of `RealtimeThread` or `NoHeapRealtimeThread` and
`t.interrupt()` or `AIE.fire()` is executed by any thread in the system then:

1. If control is in an ATC-deferred section, then the AIE is put into a pending state.
2. If control is in an AI method and not in a `try` block or a synchronized block, then
   the method from which the AI method had been invoked immediately receives
   the fired AIE without further execution of the logic in the AI method and the
   AIE's state is set to pending.
3. As with normal Java exception semantics, if control is within a `try` block
   contained within an AI method control transfers to the first statement of the
   appropriate `catch` clause. If no appropriate `catch` clause exists, then the calling
   method receives the fired AIE and the AIE's state is set to pending.
4. If control is in either `wait()`, `sleep()`, or `join()`, the thread is awakened and the
   fired AIE (which is a subclass of `InterruptedException`) is thrown. Then ATC
   follows option 1, 2, or 3 as appropriate.
5. If control is in a non-AI method, control continues normally until the first attempt
   to return to an AI method or invoke an AI method. Then ATC follows option 1, 2,
   or 3 as appropriate.
6. If control is transferred from a non-AI method to an AI method through the action
   of propagating an exception and if an AIE is pending then when the transition to
   the AI-method occurs the thrown exception is discarded and replaced by the AIE.

If an AIE is in a pending state then this AIE is thrown only when:

1. Control enters an AI-method.
2. Control returns to an AI-method.
3. Control leaves a synchronized block within an AI-method.

When happened() is called on an AIE or that AIE is superseded by another the first AIE's state is made non-pending.

An AIE may be raised while another AIE is pending or in action. Because AI code blocks are nested by method invocation (a stack-based nesting) there is a natural precedence among active instances of AIE. Let AIE_0 be the AIE raised when t.interrupt() is invoked and AIE_i (i = 1,...,n, for n unique instances of AIE) be the AIE raised when AIE_i.fire() is invoked. Assume stacks grow down and therefore the phrase "a frame lower on the stack than this frame" refers to a method at a deeper nesting level.

1. If the current AIE is an AIE_0 and the new AIE is an AIE_x associated with any frame on the stack then the new AIE (AIE_x) is discarded.
2. If the current AIE is an AIE_x and the new AIE is an AIE_0, then the current AIE (AIE_x) is replaced by the new AIE (AIE_0).
3. If the current AIE is an AIE_x and the new AIE is an AIE_y from a frame lower on the stack, then the new AIE discarded.
4. If the current AIE is an AIE_x and the new AIE is an AIE_y from a frame higher on the stack, the current AIE is replaced by the new AIE.

Non-Blocking I/O

The RTSJ will provide mechanisms and programming disciplines to allow applications to bound waiting on I/O calls. There are two cases: (1) the device on which I/O is being performed (and thus its associated stream) is no longer needed and (2) timed, non-blocking I/O (where the device and associated streams remain viable). For case 1 the RTSJ requires that when stream.close() is called on a stream, all blocked I/O calls will throw appropriate instances of IOException. Note that this requirement adds additional semantics to stream.close() which require blocked calls to throw an appropriate exception in addition to just checking for closed streams at the commencement of the I/O call. For case 2 the RTSJ recommends a programming discipline in which one thread uses the blocking calls from java.io.* and provides timed, non-blocking methods used by other threads. (See the examples in the section on asynchrony).

Rationale

The design of the asynchronous event handling was intended to provide the necessary functionality while allowing efficient implementations and catering to a variety of real-time applications. In particular, in some real-time systems there may be a large number of potential events and event handlers (numbering in the thousands or perhaps even the tens of thousands), although at any given time only a small number will be used. Thus it would not be appropriate to dedicate a thread to each event handler. The RTSJ addresses this issue by allowing the programmer to specify an event handler either as not bound to a specific thread (the class `AsyncEventHandler`) or alternatively as bound to a thread (`BoundAsyncEventHandler`).

Events are dataless: the fire method does not pass any data to the handler. This was intentional in the interest of simplicity and efficiency. An application that needs to associate data with an `AsyncEvent` can do so explicitly by setting up a buffer; it will then need to deal with buffer overflow issues as required by the application.

The ability for one thread to trigger an ATC in another thread is necessary in many kinds of real-time applications but must be designed carefully in order to minimize the risks of problems such as data structure corruption and deadlock. There is, invariably, a tension between the desire to cause an ATC to be immediate, and the desire to ensure that certain sections of code are executed to completion.

One basic decision was to allow ATC in a method only if the method explicitly permits this. The default of no ATC is reasonable, since legacy code might be written expecting no ATC, and asynchronously aborting the execution of such a method could lead to unpredictable results. Since the natural way to model ATC is with an exception (`AsynchronouslyInterruptedException`, or AIE), the way that a method indicates its susceptibility to ATC is by including AIE on its `throws` clause. Causing this exception to be thrown in a thread `t` as an effect of calling `t.interrupt()` was a natural extension of the semantics of interrupt as currently defined by `java.lang.Thread`.

One ATC-deferred section is `synchronized` code. This is a context that needs to be executed completely in order to ensure a program operates correctly. If `synchronized` code is aborted, a shared object could be left in an inconsistent state.

Constructors and `finally` clauses are subject to interruption. If a constructor is aborted, an object might be only partially initialized. If a `finally` clause is aborted, needed cleanup code might not be performed. It is the programmer's responsibility to ensure that executing these constructs does not induce unwanted ATC latency. Note that by making synchronized code ATC-deferred, this specification avoids the problems that caused `Thread.stop()` to be deprecated and that have made the use of `Thread.destroy()` prone to deadlock.

A potential problem with using the exception mechanism to model ATC is that a method with a "catch-all" handler (for example a `catch` clause identifying `Exception` or even `Throwable` as the exception class) can inadvertently intercept an exception intended for a caller. This problem is avoided by having special semantics for catching an instance of AIE. Even though a catch clause may catch an AIE, the exception will be propagated unless the handler invokes the happened method from

AIE. Thus, if a thread is asynchronously interrupted while in a try block that has a handler such as

```
catch (Throwable e){ return; }
```

then the AIE instance will still be propagated to the caller.

This specification does not provide a special mechanism for terminating a thread; ATC can be used to achieve this effect. This means that, by default, a thread cannot be terminated; it needs to invoke methods that have AIE in their throws clauses. Allowing termination as the default would have been questionable, bringing the same insecurities that are found in Thread.stop() and Thread.destroy().

9.1 AsyncEvent

Syntax: `public class AsyncEvent`

Direct Known Subclasses: `Timer`$_{112}$

An asynchronous event represents something that can happen, like a light turning red. It can have a set of handlers associated with it, and when the event occurs, the handler is scheduled by the scheduler to which it holds a reference (see AsyncEventHandler$_{127}$ and Scheduler$_{36}$).

A major motivator for this style of building events is that we expect to have lots of events and lots of event handlers. An event handler is logically very similar to a thread, but it is intended to have a much lower cost (in both time and space) — assuming that a relatively small number of events are fired and in the process of being handled at once. AsyncEvent.fire() differs from a method call because the handler (a) has scheduling parameters and (b) is executed asynchronously.

9.1.1 Constructors

```
public AsyncEvent()
```

9.1.2 Methods

```
public synchronized void addHandler(AsyncEventHandler127 handler)
```
Add a handler to the set of handlers associated with this event. An AsyncEvent may have more than one associated handler.

Parameters:

handler - The new handler to add to the list of handlers already associated with this. If handler is null then nothing happens.

Since this affects the constraints expressed in the release parameters of the existing schedulable objects, this may change the feasibility of the current schedule.

public void **bindTo**(java.lang.String happening)

Binds this to an external event (a happening). The meaningful values of happening are implementation dependent. This AsyncEvent is considered to have occurred whenever the external event occurs.

Parameters:

happening - An implementation dependent value that binds this AsyncEvent to some external event.

public ReleaseParameters$_{43}$ **createReleaseParameters**()

Create a ReleaseParameters$_{43}$ block appropriate to the timing characteristics of this event. The default is the most pessimistic: AperiodicParameters$_{47}$. This is typically called by code that is setting up a handler for this event that will fill in the parts of the release parameters that it knows the values for, like cost.

public synchronized void **fire**()

Fire (schedule the run() methods of) the handlers associated with this event.

public boolean **handledBy**(AsyncEventHandler$_{127}$ target)

Returns true if and only if this event is handled by this handler.

Parameters:

target - The handler to be tested to determine if it is associated with this. Returns false if target is null.

public synchronized void **removeHandler**(AsyncEventHandler$_{127}$ handler)

Remove a handler from the set associated with this event.

Parameters:

handler - The handler to be disassociated from this. If null nothing happens. If not already associated with this then nothing happens.

public synchronized void **setHandler**(AsyncEventHandler$_{127}$ handler)

Associate a new handler with this event, removing all existing handlers.

Since this affects the constraints expressed in the release parameters of the existing schedulable objects, this may change the feasibility of the current schedule.

Parameters:
> handler - The new and only handler to be associated with this. If handler is null then no handler will be associated with this (i.e., remove all handlers).

9.2 AsyncEventHandler

Syntax: public abstract class AsyncEventHandler implements Schedulable$_{35}$

Direct Known Subclasses: BoundAsyncEventHandler$_{132}$

All Implemented Interfaces: java.lang.Runnable, Schedulable$_{35}$

An asynchronous event handler encapsulates code that gets run at some time after an AsyncEvent$_{125}$ occurs.

It is essentially a java.lang.Runnable with a set of parameter objects, making it very much like a RealtimeThread$_{22}$. The expectation is that there may be thousands of events, with corresponding handlers, averaging about one handler per event. The number of unblocked (i.e., scheduled) handlers is expected to be relatively small.

It is guaranteed that multiple firings of an event handler will be serialized. It is also guaranteed that (unless the handler explicitly chooses otherwise) for each firing of the handler, there will be one execution of the handleAsyncEvent() method.

There is no restriction on what handlers may do. They may run for a long or short time, and they may block. (Note: blocked handlers may hold system resources.)

Normally, handlers are bound to an execution context dynamically, when their AsyncEvent$_{125}$ occurs. This can introduce a (small) time penalty. For critical handlers that can not afford the expense, and where this penalty is a problem, use a BoundAsyncEventHandler$_{132}$.

9.2.1 Constructors

public **AsyncEventHandler**()
> Create a handler whose SchedulingParameters$_{40}$ are inherited from the current thread and does not have either ReleaseParameters$_{43}$ or MemoryParameters$_{79}$.

public **AsyncEventHandler**(boolean nonheap)
> Create a handler whose parameters are inherited from the current thread, if it is a RealtimeThread$_{22}$, or null otherwise.

Parameters:

> nonheap - A flag meaning, when true, that this will have characteristics identical to a NoHeapRealtimeThread$_{26}$. A false value means this will have characteristics identical to a RealtimeThread$_{22}$. If true and the current thread is *not* a NoHeapRealtimeThread$_{26}$ or a RealtimeThread$_{22}$ executing within a ScopedMemory$_{62}$ or ImmortalMemory$_{62}$ scope then an IllegalArgumentException is thrown.

public **AsyncEventHandler**(SchedulingParameters$_{40}$ scheduling,
                    ReleaseParameters$_{43}$ release,
                    MemoryParameters$_{79}$ memory, MemoryArea$_{60}$ area,
                    ProcessingGroupParameters$_{50}$ group)

Create a handler with the specified parameters.

Parameters:

> release - A ReleaseParameters$_{43}$ object which will be associated with the constructed instance of this. If null this will have no ReleaseParameters$_{43}$.

> scheduling - A SchedulingParameters$_{40}$ object which will be associated with the constructed instance of this. If null this will be assigned the reference to the SchedulingParameters$_{40}$ of the current thread.

> memory - A MemoryParameters$_{79}$ object which will be associated with the constructed instance of this. If null this will have no MemoryParameters$_{79}$.

> area - The MemoryArea$_{60}$ for this. If null the memory area will be that of the current thread.

> group - A ProcessingGroupParameters$_{50}$ object to which this will be associated. If null this will not be associated with any processing group.

public **AsyncEventHandler**(SchedulingParameters$_{40}$ scheduling,
                    ReleaseParameters$_{43}$ release,
                    MemoryParameters$_{79}$ memory, MemoryArea$_{60}$ area,
                    ProcessingGroupParameters$_{50}$ group,
                    boolean nonheap)

Create a handler with the specified parameters.

Parameters:

> scheduling - A SchedulingParameters$_{40}$ object which will be associated with the constructed instance of this. If null this will be assigned the reference to the SchedulingParameters$_{40}$ of the current thread.

release - A ReleaseParameters$_{43}$ object which will be associated
with the constructed instance of this. If null this will have no
ReleaseParameters$_{43}$.

memory - A MemoryParameters$_{79}$ object which will be associated
with the constructed instance of this. If null this will have no
MemoryParameters$_{79}$.

area - The MemoryArea$_{60}$ for this. Must be a reference to a
ScopedMemory$_{62}$ or ImmortalMemory$_{62}$ object if noheap is true.

group - A ProcessingGroupParameters$_{50}$ object to which this will
be associated. If null this will not be associated with any
processing group.

nonheap - A flag meaning, when true, that this will have
characteristics identical to a NoHeapRealtimeThread$_{26}$.

9.2.2   Methods

public void **addToFeasibility**()

Inform the scheduler and cooperating facilities that this thread's feasibility
parameters should be considered in feasibility analysis until further
notified.

protected final synchronized int **getAndClearPendingFireCount**()

Atomically set to zero the number of pending executions of this handler
and returns the value from before it was cleared. This is used in handlers
that can handle multiple firings and that want to collapse them together.
The general form for using this is:

```
public void handleAsyncEvent() {
int fireCount = getAndClearPendingFireCount();
<handle the events>
}
```

Returns: The pending fire count.

protected synchronized int **getAndDecrementPendingFireCount**()

Atomically decrements the number of pending executions of this handler
(if it was non-zero) and returns the value from before the decrement. This
can be used in the handleAsyncEvent() method in this form to handle
multiple firings:

```
public void handleAsyncEvent() {
<setup>
do {
<handle the event>
} while(getAndDecrementPendingFireCount()>0);
}
```

This construction is necessary only in the case where one wishes to avoid the setup costs since the framework guarantees that handleAsyncEvent() will be invoked the appropriate number of times.

Returns: The pending fire count.

protected synchronized int **getAndIncrementPendingFireCount**()
Atomically increments the number of pending executions of this handler and returns the value from before the increment. The handleAsyncEvent() method does not need to do this, since the surrounding framework guarantees that the handler will be re-executed the appropriate number of times. It is only of value when there is common setup code that is expensive.

Returns: The pending fire count.

public MemoryArea$_{60}$ **getMemoryArea**()
Get the current memory area.

Returns: The current memory area in which allocations occur.

public MemoryParameters$_{79}$ **getMemoryParameters**()
Get the memory parameters associated with this handler.

Returns: The MemoryParameters$_{79}$ object associated with this.

public ProcessingGroupParameters$_{50}$ **getProcessingGroupParameters**()
Returns a reference to the ProcessingGroupParameters$_{50}$ object.

public ReleaseParameters$_{43}$ **getReleaseParameters**()
Get the release parameters associated with this handler.

Returns: The ReleaseParameters$_{43}$ object associated with this.

public Scheduler$_{36}$ **getScheduler**()
Return the Scheduler$_{36}$ for this handler.

Returns: The instance of the scheduler managing this.

public SchedulingParameters$_{40}$ **getSchedulingParameters**()
Returns a reference to the scheduling parameters object.

Returns: The SchedulingParameters$_{40}$ object associated with this.

public abstract void **handleAsyncEvent**()

> Override this method to define the action to be taken by this handler. This method will be invoked repeatedly while fireCount is greater than zero.

public void **removeFromFeasibility**()

> Inform the scheduler and cooperating facilities that this thread's feasibility parameters should not be considered in feasibility analysis until further notified.

public final void **run**()

> Used by the asynchronous event mechanism, see AsyncEvent$_{125}$. This method invokes handleAsyncEvent() repeatedly while the fire count is greater than zero. Applications cannot override this method and should thus override handleAsyncEvent() in subclasses with the logic of the handler.

public void **setMemoryParameters**(MemoryParameters$_{79}$ memory)

> Set the memory parameters associated with this handler. When it is next fired, the executing thread will use these parameters to control memory allocation. Does not affect the current invocation of the run() of this handler.

> *Parameters:*
>> memory - A MemoryParameters$_{79}$ object which will become the MemoryParameters$_{79}$ associated with this after the method call.

public void

> **setProcessingGroupParameters**(ProcessingGroupParam eters$_{50}$ parameters)

> Sets the reference to the ProcessingGroupParameters$_{50}$ object.

public void **setReleaseParameters**(ReleaseParameters$_{43}$ parameters)

> Set the release parameters associated with this handler. When it is next fired, the executing thread will use these parameters to control scheduling. If the scheduling parameters of a handler is set to null, the handler will be executed immediately when it is fired, in the thread of the firer. Does not affect the current invocation of the run() of this handler.

> Since this affects the constraints expressed in the release parameters of the existing schedulable objects, this may change the feasibility of the current schedule.

> *Parameters:*
>> parameters - A ReleaseParameters$_{43}$ object which will become the ReleaseParameters$_{43}$ associated with this after the method call.

CHAPTER 9 ASYNCHRONIZATION

public void **setScheduler**(Scheduler$_{36}$ scheduler)
> Set the scheduler for this handler. A reference to the scheduler which will manage the execution of this thread.

> *Parameters:*
>> scheduler - An instance of Scheduler$_{36}$ (or subclasses) which will manage the execution of this thread. If scheduler is null nothing happens.

> *Throws:* IllegalThreadStateException

public void **setSchedulingParameters**(SchedulingParameters$_{40}$ parameters)
> Set the scheduling parameters associated with this handler. When it is next fired, the executing thread will use these parameters to control scheduling. Does not affect the current invocation of the run() of this handler.

> *Parameters:*
>> parameters - A SchedulingParameters$_{40}$ object which will become the SchedulingParameters$_{40}$ object associated with this after the method call.

9.3   BoundAsyncEventHandler

Syntax: public abstract class BoundAsyncEventHandler extends AsyncEventHandler$_{127}$

All Implemented Interfaces: java.lang.Runnable, Schedulable$_{35}$

A bound asynchronous event handler is an asynchronous event handler that is permanently bound to a thread. Bound asynchronous event handlers are meant for use in situations where the added timeliness is worth the overhead of binding the handler to a thread.

9.3.1   Constructors

public **BoundAsyncEventHandler**()
> Create a handler whose parameters are inherited from the current thread, if it is a RealtimeThread$_{22}$, or null otherwise.

public **BoundAsyncEventHandler**(SchedulingParameters$_{40}$ scheduling, ReleaseParameters$_{43}$ release, MemoryParameters$_{79}$ memory, MemoryArea$_{60}$ area, ProcessingGroupParameters$_{50}$ group, boolean nonheap)

Create a handler with the specified ReleaseParameters$_{43}$ and
MemoryParameters$_{79}$.

Parameters:
> scheduling - A SchedulingParameters$_{40}$ object which will be
> associated with the constructed instance of this. If null this will
> be assigned the reference to the SchedulingParameters$_{40}$ of
> the current thread.
>
> release - The ReleaseParameters$_{43}$ object for this. A value of
> null will construct this without a ReleaseParameters$_{43}$ object.
>
> memory - The MemoryParameters$_{79}$ object for this. A value of null
> will construct this without a MemoryParameters$_{79}$ object.
>
> area - The MemoryArea$_{60}$ for this. Must be a reference to a
> ScopedMemory$_{62}$ or ImmortalMemory$_{62}$ object if noheap is true.
>
> nonheap - A flag meaning, when true, that this will have
> characteristics identical to a NoHeapRealtimeThread$_{26}$.
>
> group - A ProcessingGroupParameters$_{50}$ object to which this will
> be associated. If null this will not be associated with any
> processing group.

9.4   Interruptible

Syntax: public interface Interruptible

Interruptible is an interface implemented by classes that will be used as
arguments on the doInterruptible() of
AsynchronouslyInterruptedException$_{134}$ and its subclasses. doInterruptible()
invokes the implementation of the method in this interface. Thus the system can
ensure correctness before invoking run() and correctly cleaned up after run()
returns.

9.4.1   Methods

> public void **interruptAction**(AsynchronouslyInterruptedException$_{134}$
>   exception)
> This method is called by the system if the run() method is excepted. Using
> this the program logic can determine if the run() method completed
> normally or had its control asynchronously transferred to its caller.
>
> *Parameters:*
> > exception - Used to invoke methods on
> > AsynchronouslyInterruptedException$_{134}$ from within the
> > interruptAction() method.

public void **run**(AsynchronouslyInterruptedException$_{134}$ exception)
> The main piece of codc that is executed when an implemention is given to doInterruptible(). When you create a class that implements this interface (usually through an anonymous inner class) you must remember to include the throws clause to make the method interruptible. If the throws clause is omitted the run() method will not be interruptible.

> *Parameters:*
>> exception - Used to invoke methods on AsynchronouslyInterruptedException$_{134}$ from within the run() method.

> *Throws:* AsynchronouslyInterruptedException$_{134}$

9.5   AsynchronouslyInterruptedException

Syntax: public class AsynchronouslyInterruptedException extends
    java.lang.InterruptedException

Direct Known Subclasses: Timed$_{137}$

All Implemented Interfaces: java.io.Serializable

An special exception that is thrown in response to an attempt to asynchronously transfer the locus of control of a RealtimeThread$_{22}$.

When a method is declared with AsynchronouslyInterruptedException in its throws clause the platform is expected to asynchronously throw this exception if RealtimeThread.interrupt() is called while the method is executing, or if such an interrupt is pending any time control returns to the method. The interrupt is *not* thrown while any methods it invokes are executing, unless they are, in turn, declared to throw the exception. This is intended to allow long-running computations to be terminated without the overhead or latency of polling with java.lang.Thread.interrupted() .

The throws AsynchronouslyInterruptedExceptionclause is a marker on a stack frame which allows a method to be statically marked as asynchronously interruptible. Only methods that are marked this way can be interrupted.

When Thread.interrupt(), public synchronized void interrupt()$_{24}$, or this.fire() is called, the AsynchronouslyInterruptedException is compared against any currently pending AsynchronouslyInterruptedException on the thread. If there is none, or if the depth of the AsynchronouslyInterruptedException is less than the currently pending AsynchronouslyInterruptedException — i.e., it is targeted at a less deeply nested method call — it becomes the currently pending interrupt. Otherwise, it is discarded.

If the current method is interruptible, the exception is thrown on the thread. Otherwise, it just remains pending until control returns to an interruptible method, at which point the AsynchronouslyInterruptedException is thrown. When an interrupt is caught, the caller should invoke the happened() method on the AsynchronouslyInterruptedException in which it is interested to see if it matches the pending AsynchronouslyInterruptedException. If so, the pending AsynchronouslyInterruptedException is cleared from the thread. Otherwise, it will continue to propagate outward.

Thread.interrupt() and RealtimeThread.interrupt() generate a system available generic AsynchronouslyInterruptedException which will always propagate outward through interruptible methods until the generic AsynchronouslyInterruptedException is identified and stopped. Other sources (e.g., this.fire() and $Timed_{137}$) will generate a specific instance of AsynchronouslyInterruptedException which applications can identify and thus limit propogation.

9.5.1 Constructors

public **AsynchronouslyInterruptedException**()
Create an instance of AsynchronouslyInterruptedException.

9.5.2 Methods

public synchronized boolean **disable**()
Defer the throwing of this exception. If interrupt() is called when this exception is disabled, the exception is put in pending state. The exception will be thrown if this exception is subsequently enabled. This is valid only within a call to doInterruptible(). Otherwise it returns false and does nothing.

Returns: True if this is disabled otherwise returns false.

public boolean **doInterruptible**($Interruptible_{133}$ logic)
Execute the run() method of the given $Interruptible_{133}$. This method may be on the stack in exactly one $RealtimeThread_{22}$. An attempt to invoke this method in a thread while it is on the stack of another or the same thread will cause an immediate return with a value of false.

Parameters:
>   code - An instance of an Interruptible$_{133}$ whose run() method
>   will be called.

Returns: True if the method call completed normally. Returns false if
>   another call to doInterruptible has not completed.

`public synchronized boolean` **`enable`**`()`
>   Enable the throwing of this exception. This is valid only within a call to
>   doInterruptible(). Otherwise it returns false and does nothing.

Returns: True if this is enabled otherwise returns false.

`public synchronized boolean` **`fire`**`()`
>   Make this exception the current exception if doInterruptible() has been
>   invoked and not completed.

Returns: True if this was fired. If there is no current invocation of
>   doInterruptible(), then false is returned with no other effect.
>   False is also returned if there is already a current
>   doInterruptible() or if disable() has been called.

`public static AsynchronouslyInterruptedException`$_{134}$ **`getGeneric`**`()`
>   Return the system generic AsynchronouslyInterruptedException,
>   which is generated when RealtimeThread.interrupt() is invoked.

`public boolean` **`happened`**`(boolean propagate)`
>   Used with an instance of this exception to see if the current exception is
>   this exception.

Parameters:
>   propagate - Propagate the exception if true and this exception is not
>   the current one. If false, then the state of this is set to
>   nonpending (i.e., it will stop propagating).

Returns: True if this is the current exception. Returns false if this is not the
>   current exception.

`public boolean` **`isEnabled`**`()`
>   Query the enabled status of this exception.

Returns: True if this is enabled otherwise returns false.

`public void` **`propagate`**`()`
>   Cause the current exception to continue up the stack.

9.6   Timed

Syntax: `public class Timed extends AsynchronouslyInterruptedException`$_{134}$

All Implemented Interfaces: java.io.Serializable

Create a scope in a `RealtimeThread`$_{22}$ for which `interrupt()` will be called at the expiration of a timer. This timer will begin measuring time at some point between the time `doInterruptible()` is invoked and the time the `run()` method of the `Interruptible` object is invoked. Each call of `doInterruptible()` on an instance of `Timed` will restart the timer for the amount of time given in the constructor or the most recent invocation of `resetTime()`. All memory use of `Timed` occurs during construction or the first invocation of `doInterruptible()`. Subsequent invokes of `doInterruptible()` do not allocate memory.

Usage: `new Timed(T).doInterruptible(interruptible);`

9.6.1   Constructors

`public` **Timed**(`HighResolutionTime`$_{97}$ `time`)

Create an instance of `Timed` with a timer set to timeout. If the time is in the past the `AsynchronouslyInterruptedException`$_{134}$ mechanism is immediately activated.

Parameters:

`time` - The interval of time between the invocation of `doInterruptible()` and when `interrupt()` is called on `currentRealtimeThread()`. If null the `java.lang.IllegalArgumentException` is thrown.

Throws: `IllegalArgumentException`

9.6.2   Methods

`public boolean` **doInterruptible**(`Interruptible`$_{133}$ `logic`)

Execute a timeout method. Starts the timer and executes the `run()` method of the given `Interruptible`$_{133}$ object.

Overrides: `public boolean doInterruptible(Interruptible133 logic)`$_{135}$ in class `AsynchronouslyInterruptedException`$_{134}$

Parameters:

`logic` - Implements an `Interruptible`$_{133}$ `run()` method. If null nothing happens.

```
public void resetTime(HighResolutionTime₉₇ time)
```
To reschedule the timeout for the next invocation of doInterruptible().

Parameters:

> time - This can be an absolute time or a relative time. If null the
> timeout is not changed.

AsyncEvent Example

An easy way to construct event handlers is with anonymous inner classes:

```
AsyncEventHandler h = new AsyncEventHandler() {
 public void handleAsyncEvent() {
  System.out.print("The first handler ran!\n");
 }
};
```

They get associated with events by adding them to the event's handler list. There is a
slight naming issue that sometimes causes confusion: in the java.awt package (and
common gui api usage), an 'event' refers to something that *has happened*. In the
realtime package, (and common real-time system usage) an event refers to something
that *may happen* in the future. To have our handler h associated with the inputReady
event:

```
inputReady.addHandler(h);
```

Sometime in the future, the event gets fired:

```
System.out.print("Test 1\n");
inputReady.fire();
Thread.yield();
System.out.print("Fired the event\n");
```

Event handlers are like threads in that they have release, scheduling, and memory
parameters. This complicates the preceeding example: by default, handlers are created
with the same priority as the creating thread. When *inputReady* is fired, *h* becomes
runnable, but the current thread is already running. So *h* just sits in the run queue
waiting for the current process to do something that gives up the processor.

For example, we can create a low and high priority handler like this:

```
SchedulingParameters low = new PriorityParameters(
    PriorityScheduler.getMinPriority(null));
inputReady.setHandler(new AsyncEventHandler(low,null,null) {
 public void handleAsyncEvent() {
  System.out.print("The low priority handler ran!\n");
 }
});
SchedulingParameters high = new PriorityParameters(
    PriorityScheduler.getMaxPriority(null));
inputReady.addHandler(new AsyncEventHandler(high, null, null) {
 public void handleAsyncEvent() {
  System.out.print("The high priority handler ran!\n");
 }
});
```

If we fire the event off, the low priority handler doesn't run until there's some idle time on the processor:

```
System.out.print("\nTest 2\n");
inputReady.fire();
System.out.print("After the fire\n");
Thread.sleep(100);
System.out.print("After the sleep\n");
```

ReleaseParameters are somewhat problematic with respect to AsyncEvents. They encapsulate the information needed for feasibility analysis, which consists of a combination of information about when things happen and about the computation that is triggered. In the case of instances of AsyncEvent, the knowledge about those two collections of information is seperated: the event knows about when things happen, while the handler knows about the computation that is triggered. When setting up ReleaseParameters for an AsyncEvent, the following pattern should be followed:

```
ReleaseParameters rp = inputReady.createReleaseParameters();
rp.setCost(new RelativeTime(1,0));
AsyncEventHandler h2 = new AsyncEventHandler(high, rp, null){
 public void handleAsyncEvent() { System.out.print("Whatever...\n"
); }};
```

The call, inputReady.createReleaseParameters() creates a ReleaseParameters object (actually some subclass of ReleaseParameters) and populates it with information about when the event will fire. For example, if inputReady were a PeriodicTimer event, createReleaseParameters() would create a PeriodicParameters object and fill in the periodicity fields.

Output from running the example

```
Test 1
The first handler ran!
Fired the event

Test 2
The high priority handler ran!
After the fire
The low priority handler ran!
After the sleep
```

AIE Example

An AsynchronouslyInterruptedException allows code to be written so that it can be aborted in a controlled fashion in response to an action by another thread, or by an external event. A block of interruptible code is associated with the exception that can be used to terminate its execution. If the asynchronous exception is fired at any point during the execution of the interruptible code, control is transferred to the end of the executable section of code. If the interruptible code calls some other code that isn't interruptible and the exception is fired, the exception remains pending until superseded by a more pertinent exception, or until control returns to the interruptible section. In the latter case, the interruptible section is then terminated. To make a block of code interruptible by a particular asynchronous exception, it must be encapsulated in a class that implements the Interruptible interface. An instance of the class is passed to the doInterruptible() method on the AsynchronouslyInterruptedException that can interrupt the code block. This causes the run method of the interruptible object to be executed. Execution can be interrupted at any point during the run method. Note: Only one thread can be executing interruptible code within an asynchronous exception at a given time. To interrupt more than one thread it is necessary to multiplex a source, such as an AsyncEvent, to multiple asynchronous exceptions. An anonymous inner class can be used to code inline interruptible code, as in the following:

```
MyInterrupt aie = new MyInterrupt();
aie.doInterruptible(new Interruptible() {
  public void runNonInterruptible() {
    //do something that can't be interrupted
}
public void run(AsynchronouslyInterruptedException e)
  throws AsynchronouslyInterruptedException {
```

This method can be interrupted at any point in time do something "interrupt"-safe Call to a non-interruptible method. If the asynchronous exception is fired during execution of this method, it will be deferred until return from the method.

```
runNonInterruptible();
```

We can also disable the asynchronous exception for a period of time. If it is fired, it will be deferred until it's enabled again:

```
e.disable();
```

And enable it again later:

```
e.enable();
```

Upon return from run, aie can no longer effect execution of the thread.

```
public void interruptAction(AsynchronouslyInterruptedException e)
```

If we want to know whether the method was actually interrupted, we can make use of the interruptAction() entry point of the Interruptible object. This is only called if the run method was interrupted.

```
aie.doInterruptible(new Interruptible() {
  public void run(AsynchronouslyInterruptedException e)
  throws AsynchronouslyInterruptedException {
    //do something interrupt-safe
}
public void interruptAction(AsynchronouslyInterruptedException e)
{
  try {
    MyInterrupt myAie = (MyInterrupt)e;
    myAie.wasInterrupted = true;
  } catch (ClassCastException ce) {
  }
}
    //do something about it - abort or retry
}
```

AIE Example 2

In order to asynchronously interrupt code running in another thread, it is necessary to obtain a reference to the AsynchronouslyInterruptedException that the thread is expecting. This will usually be stored in a field on the thread, or may be kept in a globally accessible object. Once the reference is obtained, the other thread can be interrupted by calling the fire method on the asynchronous exception.

```
getInterrupt().fire();
```

An asynchronous exception may be bound to an event, in which case, firing the event
will result in the asynchronous exception being fired automatically. The real-time
extensions package does this to implement timed expressions, where expiration of the
timer automatically interrupts the expression:

```
(new Timed(new RelativeTime(50,0))).doInterruptible(
  new Interruptible() {
public void run(AsynchronouslyInterruptedException e) {
```

The run method will have 50 ms to execute. At the end of this time an asynchronous
exception will be fired, interrupting the run method.

```
public void interruptAction(AsynchronouslyInterruptedException e)
```

AIE Example 3

An asynchronous exception may be bound to an `AsyncEvent`. This allows a single
asynchronous event to be used to interrupt multiple threads. It also allows
implementation dependent external events (happenings) to be used to fire
asynchronous exceptions that interrupt threads.

```
class Interrupt extends AsynchronouslyInterruptedException {
  private class EventHandler extends AsyncEventHandler {
    AsyncEvent event;
    AsynchronouslyInterruptedException aie;
    public EventHandler(AsyncEvent event,
  AsynchronouslyInterruptedException aie) {
    super(new SchedulingParameters(RealtimeThread.MAX_PRIORITY),null
,null);
    this.event = event;
    this.aie = aie;
    try {
      event.addHandler(this);
    } catch (AdmissionControlException e) {
    }
    }
    public void handleAsyncEvent() {
    aie.fire();
    }
  }
  EventHandler handler;
  public Interrupt(AsyncEvent event) {
    super();
```

Create the `EventHandler` for firing the asynchronous exception.

```
handler = new EventHandler(event, this);
```

In order to asynchronously interrupt code running in another thread(s), it is necessary to obtain a reference to the AsyncEvent that has been bound to the asynchronous exceptions that those threads are expecting. Once the reference is obtained, the other threads can be interrupted by calling the fire method on the asynchronous event.

```
getInterrupt().fire();
```

For the special case of POSIX systems, this can also be initiated in response to a signal:

```
POSIXSignalHandler.addHandler(POSIXSignalHandler.SIGINT,
  new AsyncEventHandler() {
public void handleAsyncEvent() {
  AIEExample3.getInterrupt().fire();
}
  });
  }
}
```

AIE Example 4

Interruptible blocks of code can be nested. In this case the asynchronous exception of the less deeply nested interruptible block takes precedence over the more asynchronous exception of the more deeply nested block. If an asynchronous exception is "in flight" for the most deeply nested interruptible block when the other asynchronous exception is fired, the new exception supersedes the first, causing the interrupt to transfer control to the end of the outer block. An anonymous inner class can be used to code inline interruptible code, as in the following:

```
AsynchronouslyInterruptedException hiPriority =
  new AsynchronouslyInterruptedException();
hiPriority.doInterruptible(new Interruptible() {
  public void run(AsynchronouslyInterruptedException e)
throws AsynchronouslyInterruptedException {
AsynchronouslyInterruptedException loPriority =
  new AsynchronouslyInterruptedException();
```

This method can be interrupted at any point in time by the hiPriority exception

```
loPriority.doInterruptible(new Interruptible() {
  public void run(AsynchronouslyInterruptedException e)
throws AsynchronouslyInterruptedException {
```

This method can be interrupted at any point in time by either the hiPriority or the loPriority exception. In the case of the hiPriority exception, control is transferred to the end of the outer run method.

```
public void interruptAction(AsynchronouslyInterruptedException e)
```

CHAPTER **10**

System and Options

This section contains classes that:

- Provide a common idiom for binding POSIX signals to instances of `AsyncEvent` when POSIX signals are available on the underlying platform.
- Provide a class that contains operations and semantics that affect the entire system.
- Provide the security semantics required by the additional features in the entirety of this specification, which are additional to those required by implementations of the Java Language Specification.

The `RealtimeSecurity` class provides security primarily for physical memory access.

Semantics and Requirements

This list establishes the semantics and requirements that are applicable across the classes of this section. Semantics that apply to particular classes, constructors, methods, and fields will be found in the class description and the constructor, method, and field detail sections.

1. The POSIX signal handler class is required to be available when implementations of this specification execute on an underlying platform that provides POSIX signals or any subset of signals named with the POSIX names.
2. The RealtimeSecurity class is required.

Rationale

This specification accommodates the variation in underlying system variation in a number of ways. One of the most important is the concept of optionally required classes (e.g., the POSIX signal handler class). This class provides a commonality that can be relied upon by program logic that intends to execute on implementations that themselves execute on POSIX compliant systems.

The RealtimeSystem class functions in similar capacity to java.lang.System. Similarly, the RealtimeSecurity class functions similarly to java.lang.SecurityManager.

10.1   POSIXSignalHandler

Syntax: public final class POSIXSignalHandler

Use instances of AsyncEvent$_{125}$ to handle POSIX signals. Usage:

POSIXSignalHandler.addHandler(SIGINT, intHandler);

This class is required to be implemented only if the underlying operating system supports POSIX signals.

10.1.1   Fields

public static final int **SIGABRT**
    Used by abort, replace SIGIOT in the future.

public static final int **SIGALRM**
    Alarm clock.

public static final int **SIGBUS**
    Bus error.

public static final int **SIGCANCEL**
    Thread cancellation signal used by libthread.

public static final int **SIGCHLD**
    Child status change alias (POSIX).

public static final int **SIGCLD**
    Child status change.

public static final int **SIGCONT**
    Stopped process has been continued.

public static final int **SIGEMT**
    EMT instruction.

`public static final int` **SIGFPE**
Floating point exception.

`public static final int` **SIGFREEZE**
Special signal used by CPR.

`public static final int` **SIGHUP**
Hangup.

`public static final int` **SIGILL**
Illegal instruction (not reset when caught).

`public static final int` **SIGINT**
Interrupt (rubout).

`public static final int` **SIGIO**
Socket I/O possible (SIGPOLL alias).

`public static final int` **SIGIOT**
IOT instruction.

`public static final int` **SIGKILL**
Kill (cannot be caught or ignored).

`public static final int` **SIGLOST**
Resource lost (e.g., record-lock lost).

`public static final int` **SIGLWP**
Special signal used by thread library.

`public static final int` **SIGPIPE**
Write on a pipe with no one to read it.

`public static final int` **SIGPOLL**
Pollable event occured.

`public static final int` **SIGPROF**
Profiling timer expired.

`public static final int` **SIGPWR**
Power-fail restart.

`public static final int` **SIGQUIT**
Quit (ASCII FS).

`public static final int` **SIGSEGV**
Segmentation violation.

`public static final int` **SIGSTOP**
Stop (cannot be caught or ignored).

`public static final int` **SIGSYS**
Bad argument to system call.

```
public static final int SIGTERM
```
Software termination signal from kill.

```
public static final int SIGTHAW
```
Special signal used by CPR.

```
public static final int SIGTRAP
```
Trace trap (not reset when caught).

```
public static final int SIGTSTP
```
User stop requested from tty.

```
public static final int SIGTTIN
```
Background tty read attempted.

```
public static final int SIGTTOU
```
Background tty write attempted.

```
public static final int SIGURG
```
Urgent socket condition.

```
public static final int SIGUSR1
```
User defined signal = 1.

```
public static final int SIGUSR2
```
User defined signal = 2.

```
public static final int SIGVTALRM
```
Virtual timer expired.

```
public static final int SIGWAITING
```
Process's lwps are blocked.

```
public static final int SIGWINCH
```
Window size change.

```
public static final int SIGXCPU
```
Exceeded cpu limit.

```
public static final int SIGXFSZ
```
Exceeded file size limit.

10.1.2 Methods

```
public static synchronized void addHandler(int signal,
                AsyncEventHandler_127 handler)
```
Add the given $AsyncEventHandler_{127}$ to the list of handlers of the $AsyncEvent_{125}$ of the given signal.

Parameters:

`signal` - One of the POSIX signals from this (e.g., `this.SIGLOST`).

handler - An AsyncEventHandler$_{127}$ which will be scheduled when the given signal occurs.

`public static synchronized void` **removeHandler**`(int signal, AsyncEventHandler`$_{127}$ `handler)`
Remove the given AsyncEventHandler$_{127}$ to the list of handlers of the AsyncEvent$_{125}$ of the given signal.

Parameters:
signal - One of the POSIX signals from this (e.g., `this.SIGLOST`).
handler - An AsyncEventHandler$_{127}$ which will be scheduled when the given signal occurs.

`public static synchronized void` **setHandler**`(int signal, AsyncEventHandler`$_{127}$ `handler)`
Set the given AsyncEventHandler$_{127}$ as the handler of the AsyncEvent$_{125}$ of the given signal.

Parameters:
signal - One of the POSIX signals from this (e.g., `this.SIGLOST`).
handler - An AsyncEventHandler$_{127}$ which will be scheduled when the given signal occurs. If h is null then no handler will be associated with this (i.e., remove all handlers).

10.2 RealtimeSecurity

Syntax: `public class RealtimeSecurity`

Security policy object for real-time specific issues. Primarily used to control access to physical memory.

10.2.1 Constructors

`public` **RealtimeSecurity**`()`

10.2.2 Methods

`public void` **checkAccessPhysical**`()`
Check whether the application is allowed to access physical memory.

Throws: `SecurityException` - the application doesn't have permission.

`public void` **checkAccessPhysicalRange**`(long base, longsize)`
Check whether the application is allowed to access physical memory within the specified range.

Throws: SecurityException - the application doesn't have permission.

public void **checkSetFactory**()
> Check whether the application is allowed to set factory objects.

> *Throws:* SecurityException - the application doesn't have permission.

public void **checkSetScheduler**()
> Check whether the application is allowed to set the scheduler.

> *Throws:* SecurityException - the application doesn't have permission.

10.3   RealtimeSystem

Syntax: public class RealtimeSystem

RealtimeSystem provides a means for tuning the behavior of the implementation by specifying parameters such as the maximum number of locks that can be in use concurrently, and the monitor control policy. In addition, RealtimeSystem provides a mechanism for obtaining access to the security manager, garbage collector and scheduler, to make queries from them or to set parameters.

10.3.1   Fields

public static final byte **BIG_ENDIAN**

public static final byte **BYTE_ORDER**

public static final byte **LITTLE_ENDIAN**

10.3.2   Methods

public static GarbageCollector$_{81}$ **currentGC**()
> Return a reference to the currently active garbage collector for the heap.

> *Returns:* A GarbageCollector$_{81}$ object which is the current collector collecting objects on the traditional Java heap.

public int **getConcurrentLocksUsed**()
> Get the maximum number of locks that have been used concurrently. This value can be used for tuning the concurrent locks parameter, which is used as a hint by systems that use a monitor cache.

> *Returns:* An int whose value is the number of locks in use at the time of the invocation of the method.

public int **getMaximumConcurrentLocks**()

Get the maximum number of locks that can be used concurrently without incurring an execution time increase as set by the setMaximumConcurrentLocks() methods.

Returns: An int whose value is the maximum number of locks that can be in simultaneous use.

public static RealtimeSecurity$_{149}$ **getSecurityManager**()
Get a reference to the security manager used to control access to real-time system features such as access to physical memory.

Returns: A RealtimeSecurity$_{149}$ object representing the default real-time security manager.

public void **setMaximumConcurrentLocks**(int number)
Set the anticipated maximum number of locks that may be held or waited on concurrently. Provide a hint to systems that use a monitor cache as to how much space to dedicate to the cache.

Parameters:
> number - An integer whose value becomes the number of locks that can be in simultaneous use without incurring an execution time increase. If number is less than or equal to zero nothing happens.

public void **setMaximumConcurrentLocks**(int number, boolean hard)
Set the anticipated maximum number of locks that may be held or waited on concurrently. Provide a limit for the size of the monitor cache on systems that provide one if hard is true.

Parameters:
> number - The maximum number of locks that can be in simultaneous use without incurring an execution time increase. If number is less than or equal to zero nothing happens.
> hard - If true, number sets a limit. If a lock is attempted which would cause the number of locks to exceed number then a ResourceLimitError$_{156}$ is thrown.

public static void **setSecurityManager**(RealtimeSecurity$_{149}$ manager)
Set a new real-time security manager.

Parameters:
> manager - A RealtimeSecurity$_{149}$ object which will become the new security manager.

Throws: SecurityException - Thrown if security manager has already been set.

CHAPTER **11**

Exceptions

This section contains classes that:

- Add additional exception classes required by the entirety of the other sections of this specification.
- Provide for the ability to asynchronously transfer the control of program logic.

Semantics and Requirements

This list establishes the semantics and requirements that are applicable across the classes of this section. Semantics that apply to particular classes, constructors, methods, and fields will be found in the class description and the constructor, method, and field detail sections.

1. All classes in this section are required.
2. All exceptions, except `AsynchronouslyInterruptedException`, are required to have semantics exactly as those of their eventual superclass in the `java.*` hierarchy.
3. Instances of the class `AsynchronouslyInterruptedException` can be generated by execution of program logic and by internal virtual machine mechanisms that are asynchronous to the execution of program logic which is the target of the exception.
4. Program logic that exists in methods that throw `AsynchronouslyInterruptedException` is subject to receiving an instance of `AsynchronouslyInterruptedException` at any time during execution.

Rationale

The need for additional exceptions given the new semantics added by the other sections of this specification is obvious. That the specification attaches new, nontraditional, exception semantics to `AsynchronouslyInterruptedException` is, perhaps, not so obvious. However, after careful thought, and given our self-imposed directive that only well-defined code blocks would be subject to having their control asynchronously transferred, the chosen mechanism is logical.

11.1 IllegalAssignmentError

Syntax: `public class IllegalAssignmentError extends java.lang.Error`

All Implemented Interfaces: java.io.Serializable

The exception thrown on an attempt to make an illegal assignment. For example, this will be thrown if logic attempts to assign a reference to an object in `ScopedMemory`$_{62}$ to a field in an object in `ImmortalMemory`$_{62}$.

11.1.1 Constructors

`public IllegalAssignmentError()`
　　A constructor for `IllegalAssignmentError`.

`public IllegalAssignmentError(java.lang.String description)`
　　A descriptive constructor for `IllegalAssignmentError`.

　　Parameters:
　　　　`description` - Description of the error.

11.2 MemoryAccessError

Syntax: `public class MemoryAccessError extends java.lang.Error`

All Implemented Interfaces: java.io.Serializable

The exception thrown on an attempt to refer to an object in an inaccessible `MemoryArea`$_{60}$. For example this will be thrown if logic in a `NoHeapRealtimeThread`$_{26}$ attempts to refer to an object in the traditional Java heap.

11.2.1 Constructors

public **MemoryAccessError**()
> A constructor for MemoryAccessError.

public **MemoryAccessError**(java.lang.String description)
> A descriptive constructor for MemoryAccessError.

> *Parameters:*
>> description - Description of the error.

11.3 MemoryScopeException

Syntax: public class MemoryScopeException extends java.lang.Exception

All Implemented Interfaces: java.io.Serializable

Thrown if construction of any of the wait-free queues is attempted with the ends of the queues in incompatible memory areas.

11.3.1 Constructors

public **MemoryScopeException**()
> A constructor for MemoryScopeException.

public **MemoryScopeException**(java.lang.String description)
> A descriptive constructor for MemoryScopeException.

> *Parameters:*
>> description - A description of the exception.

11.4 OffsetOutOfBoundsException

Syntax: public class OffsetOutOfBoundsException extends
java.lang.Exception

All Implemented Interfaces: java.io.Serializable

Thrown if the constructor of a ImmortalPhysicalMemory$_{69}$, ScopedPhysicalMemory$_{71}$, RawMemoryFloatAccess$_{76}$, or RawMemoryAccess$_{72}$ is given an invalid address.

11.4.1   Constructors

public **OffsetOutOfBoundsException**()
>   A constructor for OffsetOutOfBoundsException.

public **OffsetOutOfBoundsException**(java.lang.String description)
>   A descriptive constructor for OffsetOutOfBoundsException.

>   *Parameters:*
>>   description - A description of the exception.

11.5   ResourceLimitError

Syntax: public abstract class ResourceLimitError extends java.lang.Error

All Implemented Interfaces: java.io.Serializable

Thrown if an attempt is made to exceed a system resource limit, such as the maximum number of locks.

11.5.1   Constructors

public **ResourceLimitError**()
>   A constructor for ResourceLimitError.

public **ResourceLimitError**(java.lang.String description)
>   A descriptive constructor for ResourceLimitError.

>   *Parameters:*
>>   description - The description of the exception.

11.6   SizeOutOfBoundsException

Syntax: public class SizeOutOfBoundsException extends java.lang.Exception

All Implemented Interfaces: java.io.Serializable

Thrown if the constructor of a ImmortalPhysicalMemory$_{69}$, ScopedPhysicalMemory$_{71}$, RawMemoryFloatAccess$_{76}$, or RawMemoryAccess$_{72}$ is given an invalid size or if an accessor method on one of the above classes would cause access to an invalid address.

11.6.1 Constructors

public **SizeOutOfBoundsException**()
>   A constructor for SizeOutOfBoundsException.

public **SizeOutOfBoundsException**(java.lang.String description)
>   A descriptive constructor for a SizeOutOfBoundsException.

> *Parameters:*
> >   description - The description of the exception.

11.7   ThrowBoundaryError

Syntax: public class ThrowBoundaryError extends java.lang.Error

All Implemented Interfaces: java.io.Serializable

The error thrown by public void enter(java.lang.Runnable logic)$_{64}$ when a java.lang.Throwable allocated from memory that is not usable in the surrounding scope tries to propagate out of the scope of the public void enter(java.lang.Runnable logic)$_{64}$.

11.7.1 Constructors

public **ThrowBoundaryError**()
>   A constructor for ThrowBoundaryError.

public **ThrowBoundaryError**(java.lang.String description)
>   A descriptive constructor for ThrowBoundaryError.

> *Parameters:*
> >   description - Description of the error.

11.8   UnsupportedPhysicalMemoryException

Syntax: public class UnsupportedPhysicalMemoryException extends
       java.lang.Exception

All Implemented Interfaces: java.io.Serializable

Thrown when the underlying hardware does not support the type of physical memory given to the physical memory create() method. See: RawMemoryAccess$_{72}$ RawMemoryFloatAccess$_{76}$ ImmortalPhysicalMemory$_{69}$ ScopedPhysicalMemory$_{71}$

11.8.1   Constructors

public **UnsupportedPhysicalMemoryException**()
> A constructor for UnsupportedPhysicalMemoryException.

public **UnsupportedPhysicalMemoryException**(java.lang.String
> description)
> A descriptive constructor for a UnsupportedPhysicalMemoryException

> *Parameters:*
>> description - The description of the exception.

160

LEGEND

The following is a very condensed summary of all of the classes defined in this specification, listed alphabetically. It is done in the style introduced by Patrick Chan in his excellent *Java Developers Almanac*.

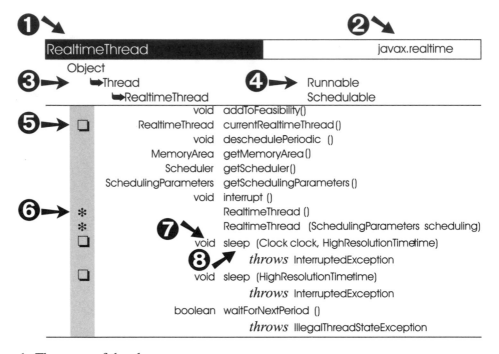

1. The name of the class.
2. The name of the package containing the class
3. The chain of superclasses. Each class is a subclass of the one above it.
4. The names of the interfaces implemented by each class.
5. A static method.
6. A constructor. Other icons that may occur in this table are:
   - ○   abstract
   - ●   final
   - ■   static final
   - ©   protected
   - ✍   field
7. The return type of a method or the declared type of an instance variable.
8. The name of the class member. If it is a method, the parameter list and optional throws clause follows. Members are arranged alphabetically.

CHAPTER 12

Almanac

AbsoluteTime	javax.realtime

```
Object
  ➡HighResolutionTime                    Comparable
     ➡AbsoluteTime
```

	AbsoluteTime **absolute**(Clock clock, AbsoluteTime destination)
✳	**AbsoluteTime**()
✳	**AbsoluteTime**(AbsoluteTime time)
✳	**AbsoluteTime**(java.util.Date date)
✳	**AbsoluteTime**(long millis, int nanos)
	AbsoluteTime **add**(long millis, int nanos)
	AbsoluteTime **add**(long millis, int nanos, AbsoluteTime destination)
●	AbsoluteTime **add**(RelativeTime time)
	AbsoluteTime **add**(RelativeTime time, AbsoluteTime destination)
	java.util.Date **getDate**()
	void **set**(java.util.Date date)
●	RelativeTime **subtract**(AbsoluteTime time)
	RelativeTime **subtract**(AbsoluteTime time, RelativeTime destination)
●	AbsoluteTime **subtract**(RelativeTime time)
	AbsoluteTime **subtract**(RelativeTime time, AbsoluteTime destination)
	String **toString**()

161

AperiodicParameters   javax.realtime

```
Object
    ➥ReleaseParameters
        ➥AperiodicParameters
```

✳	**AperiodicParameters**(RelativeTime cost, RelativeTime deadline, AsyncEventHandler overrunHandler, AsyncEventHandler missHandler)

AsyncEvent   javax.realtime

```
Object
    ➥AsyncEvent
```

	void	**addHandler**(AsyncEventHandler handler)
✳		**AsyncEvent**()
	ReleaseParameters	**createReleaseParameters**()
	void	**fire**()
	boolean	**handledBy**(AsyncEventHandler target)
	void	**removeHandler**(AsyncEventHandler handler)
	void	**setHandler**(AsyncEventHandler handler)

AsyncEventHandler   javax.realtime

```
Object
    ➥AsyncEventHandler                    Schedulable
```

	void	**addToFeasibility**()
✳		**AsyncEventHandler**()
✳		**AsyncEventHandler**(boolean nonheap)
✳		**AsyncEventHandler**(SchedulingParameters scheduling, ReleaseParameters release, MemoryParameters memory, MemoryArea area, ProcessingGroupParameters group)
✳		**AsyncEventHandler**(SchedulingParameters scheduling, ReleaseParameters release, MemoryParameters memory, MemoryArea area, ProcessingGroupParameters group, boolean nonheap)
●◆	int	**getAndClearPendingFireCount**()
◆	int	**getAndDecrementPendingFireCount**()
◆	int	**getAndIncrementPendingFireCount**()
	MemoryArea	**getMemoryArea**()
	MemoryParameters	**getMemoryParameters**()
	ProcessingGroupParameters	**getProcessingGroupParameters**()
	ReleaseParameters	**getReleaseParameters**()
	Scheduler	**getScheduler**()

	SchedulingParameters	**getSchedulingParameters**()
○	void	**handleAsyncEvent**()
	void	**removeFromFeasibility**()
●	void	**run**()
	void	**setMemoryParameters**(MemoryParameters memory)
	void	**setProcessingGroupParameters**(ProcessingGroupParameters parameters)
	void	**setReleaseParameters**(ReleaseParameters parameters)
	void	**setScheduler**(Scheduler scheduler) *throws* IllegalThreadStateException
	void	**setSchedulingParameters**(SchedulingParameters parameters)

AsynchronouslyInterruptedException   javax.realtime

```
Object
  ➥Throwable                        java.io.Serializable
     ➥Exception
        ➥InterruptedException
           ➥AsynchronouslyInterruptedException
```

✳		**AsynchronouslyInterruptedException**()
	boolean	**disable**()
	boolean	**doInterruptible**(Interruptible logic)
	boolean	**enable**()
	boolean	**fire**()
❏	AsynchronouslyInterruptedException	**getGeneric**()
	boolean	**happened**(boolean propagate)
	boolean	**isEnabled**()
	void	**propagate**()

BoundAsyncEventHandler   javax.realtime

```
Object
  ➥AsyncEventHandler                Schedulable
     ➥BoundAsyncEventHandler
```

✳	**BoundAsyncEventHandler**()
✳	**BoundAsyncEventHandler**(SchedulingParameters scheduling, ReleaseParameters release, MemoryParameters memory, MemoryArea area, ProcessingGroupParameters group, boolean nonheap)

Clock   `javax.realtime`

Object
  ➥Clock

✳		**Clock**()
❑	Clock	**getRealtimeClock**()
○	RelativeTime	**getResolution**()
	AbsoluteTime	**getTime**()
○	void	**getTime**(AbsoluteTime time)
○	void	**setResolution**(RelativeTime resolution)

GarbageCollector   `javax.realtime`

Object
  ➥GarbageCollector

✳		**GarbageCollector**()
○	RelativeTime	**getPreemptionLatency**()

HeapMemory   `javax.realtime`

Object
  ➥MemoryArea
     ➥HeapMemory

❑	HeapMemory	**instance**()

HighResolutionTime   `javax.realtime`

Object
  ➥HighResolutionTime   Comparable

○	AbsoluteTime	**absolute**(Clock clock, AbsoluteTime dest)
	int	**compareTo**(HighResolutionTime time)
	int	**compareTo**(Object object)
	boolean	**equals**(HighResolutionTime time)
	boolean	**equals**(Object object)
●	long	**getMilliseconds**()
●	int	**getNanoseconds**()
	int	**hashCode**()
	void	**set**(HighResolutionTime time)
	void	**set**(long millis)
	void	**set**(long millis, int nanos)

IllegalAssignmentError   `javax.realtime`

```
Object
    ➥Throwable                              java.io.Serializable
        ➥Error
            ➥IllegalAssignmentError
```

✱	**IllegalAssignmentError**()
✱	**IllegalAssignmentError**(String description)

ImmortalMemory   `javax.realtime`

```
Object
    ➥MemoryArea
        ➥ImmortalMemory
```

❑	ImmortalMemory **instance**()

ImmortalPhysicalMemory   `javax.realtime`

```
Object
    ➥MemoryArea
        ➥ImmortalPhysicalMemory
```

❑	ImmortalPhysicalMemory	**create**(Object type, long size) *throws* SecurityException, SizeOutOfBoundsException, UnsupportedPhysicalMemoryException
❑	ImmortalPhysicalMemory	**create**(Object type, long base, long size) *throws* SecurityException, SizeOutOfBoundsException, OffsetOutOfBoundsException, UnsupportedPhysicalMemoryException
✱◆		**ImmortalPhysicalMemory**(ImmortalPhysicalMemory memory, long base, long size)
✱◆		**ImmortalPhysicalMemory**(long base, longsize)
❑		void **setFactory**(PhysicalMemoryFactory factory)

ImportanceParameters   `javax.realtime`

```
Object
    ➥SchedulingParameters
        ➥PriorityParameters
            ➥ImportanceParameters
```

	int **getImportance**()
✱	**ImportanceParameters**(int priority, int importance)
	void **setImportance**(int importance)
	String **toString**()

Interruptible   javax.realtime

Interruptible

	void **interruptAction**(AsynchronouslyInterruptedException exception)
	void **run**(AsynchronouslyInterruptedException exception) *throws* AsynchronouslyInterruptedException

LTMemory   javax.realtime

Object
➡️MemoryArea
   ➡️ScopedMemory
      ➡️LTMemory

✳	**LTMemory**(long initialSizeInBytes, long maxSizeInBytes)

MemoryAccessError   javax.realtime

Object
➡️Throwable   java.io.Serializable
   ➡️Error
      ➡️MemoryAccessError

✳	**MemoryAccessError**()
✳	**MemoryAccessError**(String description)

MemoryArea   javax.realtime

Object
➡️MemoryArea

	void **enter**(Runnable logic)
❑	MemoryArea **getMemoryArea**(Object object)
✳◆	**MemoryArea**(long sizeInBytes)
	long **memoryConsumed**()
	long **memoryRemaining**()
	Object **newArray**(Class type, int number) *throws* InstantiationException, IllegalAccessException
	Object **newInstance**(Class type) *throws* InstantiationException, IllegalAccessException
	long **size**()

MemoryParameters `javax.realtime`

```
Object
    ➥MemoryParameters
```

	long	**getAllocationRate**()
	long	**getMaxImmortal**()
	long	**getMaxMemoryArea**()
✳		**MemoryParameters**(long maxMemoryArea, long maxImmortal) *throws* IllegalArgumentException
✳		**MemoryParameters**(long maxMemoryArea, long maxImmortal, long allocationRate) *throws* IllegalArgumentException
✎■	long	**NO_MAX**
	void	**setAllocationRate**(long rate)
	boolean	**setMaxImmortal**(long maximum)
	boolean	**setMaxMemoryArea**(long maximum)

MemoryScopeException `javax.realtime`

```
Object
    ➥Throwable                    java.io.Serializable
        ➥Exception
            ➥MemoryScopeException
```

✳	**MemoryScopeException**()
✳	**MemoryScopeException**(String description)

MonitorControl `javax.realtime`

```
Object
    ➥MonitorControl
```

✳		**MonitorControl**()
❑	void	**setMonitorControl**(MonitorControl policy)
❑	void	**setMonitorControl**(Object monitor, MonitorControl policy)

NoHeapRealtimeThread   javax.realtime

```
Object
  ➡Thread                                    Runnable
     ➡RealtimeThread                         Schedulable
        ➡NoHeapRealtimeThread
```

✳	**NoHeapRealtimeThread**(SchedulingParameters scheduling, MemoryArea area) *throws* IllegalArgumentException
✳	**NoHeapRealtimeThread**(SchedulingParameters scheduling, ReleaseParameters release, MemoryArea area) *throws* IllegalArgumentException
✳	**NoHeapRealtimeThread**(SchedulingParameters scheduling, ReleaseParameters release, MemoryParameters memory, MemoryArea area, ProcessingGroupParameters group, Runnable logic) *throws* IllegalArgumentException
✎▪	int **NORM_PRIORITY**

OffsetOutOfBoundsException   javax.realtime

```
Object
  ➡Throwable                                 java.io.Serializable
     ➡Exception
        ➡OffsetOutOfBoundsException
```

✳	**OffsetOutOfBoundsException**()
✳	**OffsetOutOfBoundsException**(String description)

OneShotTimer   javax.realtime

```
Object
  ➡AsyncEvent
     ➡Timer
        ➡OneShotTimer
```

✳	**OneShotTimer**(HighResolutionTime time, AsyncEventHandler handler)
✳	**OneShotTimer**(HighResolutionTime start, Clock clock, AsyncEventHandler handler)

PeriodicParameters   `javax.realtime`

```
Object
    ➥ReleaseParameters
        ➥PeriodicParameters
```

	RelativeTime **getPeriod**()
	HighResolutionTime **getStart**()
✳	**PeriodicParameters**(HighResolutionTime start, RelativeTime period, RelativeTime cost, RelativeTime deadline, AsyncEventHandler overrunHandler, AsyncEventHandler missHandler)
	void **setPeriod**(RelativeTime period)
	void **setStart**(HighResolutionTime start)

PeriodicTimer   `javax.realtime`

```
Object
    ➥AsyncEvent
        ➥Timer
            ➥PeriodicTimer
```

	ReleaseParameters **createReleaseParameters**()
	void **fire**()
	AbsoluteTime **getFireTime**()
	RelativeTime **getInterval**()
✳	**PeriodicTimer**(HighResolutionTime start, RelativeTime interval, AsyncEventHandler handler)
✳	**PeriodicTimer**(HighResolutionTime start, RelativeTime interval, Clock clock, AsyncEventHandler handler)
	void **setInterval**(RelativeTime interval)

PhysicalMemoryFactory   `javax.realtime`

```
Object
    ➥PhysicalMemoryFactory
```

🔒■	String **ALIGNED**
🔒■	String **BYTESWAP**
◆	Object **create**(Object memoryType, Class physMemType, long base, long size)
🔒■	String **DMA**
◆	long **getTypedMemoryBase**(Object memoryType, long size)
🔒■	String **SHARED**

POSIXSignalHandler `javax.realtime`

Object
➥POSIXSignalHandler

❑	void **addHandler**(int signal, AsyncEventHandler handler)
❑	void **removeHandler**(int signal, AsyncEventHandler handler)
❑	void **setHandler**(int signal, AsyncEventHandler handler)
✍■	int **SIGABRT**
✍■	int **SIGALRM**
✍■	int **SIGBUS**
✍■	int **SIGCANCEL**
✍■	int **SIGCHLD**
✍■	int **SIGCLD**
✍■	int **SIGCONT**
✍■	int **SIGEMT**
✍■	int **SIGFPE**
✍■	int **SIGFREEZE**
✍■	int **SIGHUP**
✍■	int **SIGILL**
✍■	int **SIGINT**
✍■	int **SIGIO**
✍■	int **SIGIOT**
✍■	int **SIGKILL**
✍■	int **SIGLOST**
✍■	int **SIGLWP**
✍■	int **SIGPIPE**
✍■	int **SIGPOLL**
✍■	int **SIGPROF**
✍■	int **SIGPWR**
✍■	int **SIGQUIT**
✍■	int **SIGSEGV**
✍■	int **SIGSTOP**
✍■	int **SIGSYS**
✍■	int **SIGTERM**
✍■	int **SIGTHAW**
✍■	int **SIGTRAP**
✍■	int **SIGTSTP**
✍■	int **SIGTTIN**
✍■	int **SIGTTOU**
✍■	int **SIGURG**
✍■	int **SIGUSR1**
✍■	int **SIGUSR2**

	int **SIGVTALRM**
✍■	int **SIGWAITING**
✍■	int **SIGWINCH**
✍■	int **SIGXCPU**
✍■	int **SIGXFSZ**

PriorityCeilingEmulation   javax.realtime

Object
  ➥MonitorControl
    ➥PriorityCeilingEmulation

	int **getDefaultCeiling**()
✳	**PriorityCeilingEmulation**(int ceiling)

PriorityInheritance   javax.realtime

Object
  ➥MonitorControl
    ➥PriorityInheritance

❑	PriorityInheritance **instance**()
✳	**PriorityInheritance**()

PriorityParameters   javax.realtime

Object
  ➥SchedulingParameters
    ➥PriorityParameters

	int **getPriority**()
✳	**PriorityParameters**(int priority)
	void **setPriority**(int priority) *throws* IllegalArgumentException
	String **toString**()

PriorityScheduler   javax.realtime

Object
  ➥Scheduler
    ➥PriorityScheduler

	void **addToFeasibility**(Schedulable s)
	boolean **changeIfFeasible**(Schedulable schedulable, ReleaseParameters release, MemoryParameters memory)
	void **fireSchedulable**(Schedulable schedulable)
	int **getMaxPriority**()
❑	int **getMaxPriority**(Thread thread)

	int	**getMinPriority**()
❑	int	**getMinPriority**(Thread thread)
	int	**getNormPriority**()
❑	int	**getNormPriority**(Thread thread)
	String	**getPolicyName**()
❑	PriorityScheduler	**instance**()
	boolean	**isFeasible**()
✳		**PriorityScheduler**()
◆	void	**removeFromFeasibility**(Schedulable s)

ProcessingGroupParameters

javax.realtime

Object
→ProcessingGroupParameters

	RelativeTime	**getCost**()
	AsyncEventHandler	**getCostOverrunHandler**()
	RelativeTime	**getDeadline**()
	AsyncEventHandler	**getDeadlineMissHandler**()
	RelativeTime	**getPeriod**()
	HighResolutionTime	**getStart**()
✳		**ProcessingGroupParameters**(HighResolutionTime start, RelativeTime period, RelativeTime cost, RelativeTime deadline, AsyncEventHandler overrunHandler, AsyncEventHandler missHandler)
	void	**setCost**(RelativeTime cost)
	void	**setCostOverrunHandler**(AsyncEventHandler handler)
	void	**setDeadline**(RelativeTime deadline)
	void	**setDeadlineMissHandler**(AsyncEventHandler handler)
	void	**setPeriod**(RelativeTime period)
	void	**setStart**(HighResolutionTime start)

RationalTime

javax.realtime

Object
→HighResolutionTime   Comparable
→RelativeTime
→RationalTime

	AbsoluteTime	**absolute**(Clock clock, AbsoluteTime destination)
	void	**addInterarrivalTo**(AbsoluteTime destination)
	int	**getFrequency**()
	RelativeTime	**getInterarrivalTime**(RelativeTime dest)
✳		**RationalTime**(int frequency)
✳		**RationalTime**(int frequency, longmillis, int nanos) *throws* IllegalArgumentException

✳	**RationalTime**(int frequency, RelativeTimeinterval)
	void **set**(long millis, int nanos) *throws* IllegalArgumentException
	void **setFrequency**(int frequency)

RawMemoryAccess   `javax.realtime`

Object
   ➥RawMemoryAccess

❏	RawMemoryAccess	**create**(Object type, long size) *throws* SecurityException, OffsetOutOfBoundsException, SizeOutOfBoundsException, UnsupportedPhysicalMemoryException
❏	RawMemoryAccess	**create**(Object type, long base, long size) *throws* SecurityException, OffsetOutOfBoundsException, SizeOutOfBoundsException, UnsupportedPhysicalMemoryException
	byte	**getByte**(long offset) *throws* OffsetOutOfBoundsException, SizeOutOfBoundsException
	void	**getBytes**(long offset, byte[] bytes, int low, int number) *throws* OffsetOutOfBoundsException, SizeOutOfBoundsException
	int	**getInt**(long offset) *throws* OffsetOutOfBoundsException, SizeOutOfBoundsException
	void	**getInts**(long offset, int[] ints, int low, int number) *throws* OffsetOutOfBoundsException, SizeOutOfBoundsException
	long	**getLong**(long offset) *throws* OffsetOutOfBoundsException, SizeOutOfBoundsException
	void	**getLongs**(long offset, long[] longs, int low, int number) *throws* OffsetOutOfBoundsException, SizeOutOfBoundsException
	long	**getMappedAddress**()
	short	**getShort**(long offset) *throws* OffsetOutOfBoundsException, SizeOutOfBoundsException
	void	**getShorts**(long offset, short[] shorts, int low, int number) *throws* OffsetOutOfBoundsException, SizeOutOfBoundsException
	long	**map**()
	long	**map**(long base)
	long	**map**(long base, long size)
✳◆		**RawMemoryAccess**(long base, long size)
✳◆		**RawMemoryAccess**(RawMemoryAccess memory, long base, long size)
	void	**setByte**(long offset, byte value) *throws* OffsetOutOfBoundsException, SizeOutOfBoundsException

```
               void setBytes(long offset, byte[] bytes, int low,
                        int number)
                        throws OffsetOutOfBoundsException, SizeOutOf-
                        BoundsException
               void setInt(long offset, int value)
                        throws OffsetOutOfBoundsException, SizeOutOf-
                        BoundsException
               void setInts(long offset, int[] ints, int low,
                        int number)
                        throws OffsetOutOfBoundsException, SizeOutOf-
                        BoundsException
               void setLong(long offset, long value)
                        throws OffsetOutOfBoundsException, SizeOutOf-
                        BoundsException
               void setLongs(long offset, long[] longs, int low,
                        int n) throws OffsetOutOfBoundsException,
                        SizeOutOfBoundsException
               void setShort(long offset, short value)
                        throws OffsetOutOfBoundsException, SizeOutOf-
                        BoundsException
               void setShorts(long offset, short[] shorts, int low,
                        int number)
                        throws OffsetOutOfBoundsException, SizeOutOf-
                        BoundsException
               void unmap()
```

RawMemoryFloatAccess   javax.realtime

```
Object
    ➡RawMemoryAccess
        ➡RawMemoryFloatAccess
```

```
❑    RawMemoryFloatAccess createFloatAccess(Object type, long size)
                        throws SecurityException, OffsetOutOfBound-
                        sException, SizeOutOfBoundsException, Unsup-
                        portedPhysicalMemoryException
❑    RawMemoryFloatAccess createFloatAccess(Object type, long base,
                        long size) throws SecurityException, Off-
                        setOutOfBoundsException, SizeOutOfBoundsEx-
                        ception, UnsupportedPhysicalMemoryException
               byte getDouble(long offset)
                        throws OffsetOutOfBoundsException, SizeOutOf-
                        BoundsException
               void getDoubles(long offset, double[] doubless,
                        int low, int number)
                        throws OffsetOutOfBoundsException, SizeOutOf-
                        BoundsException
               byte getFloat(long offset)
                        throws OffsetOutOfBoundsException, SizeOutOf-
                        BoundsException
               void getFloats(long offset, float[] floats, int low,
                        int number)
                        throws OffsetOutOfBoundsException, SizeOutOf-
                        BoundsException
❋◆             RawMemoryFloatAccess(long base, long size)
❋◆             RawMemoryFloatAccess(RawMemoryAccess memory,
                        long base, longsize)
               void setDouble(long offset, double value)
                        throws OffsetOutOfBoundsException, SizeOutOf-
                        BoundsException
```

```
                                    void setDoubles(long offset, double[] doubles, int low,
                                             int number)
                                             throws OffsetOutOfBoundsException, SizeOutOf-
                                             BoundsException
                                    void setFloat(long offset, float value)
                                             throws OffsetOutOfBoundsException, SizeOutOf-
                                             BoundsException
                                    void setFloats(long offset, float[] floats, int low,
                                             int number)
                                             throws OffsetOutOfBoundsException, SizeOutOf-
                                             BoundsException
```

RealtimeSecurity   javax.realtime

Object
  ➡RealtimeSecurity

	void	**checkAccessPhysical**() *throws* SecurityException
	void	**checkAccessPhysicalRange**(long base, long size) *throws* SecurityException
	void	**checkSetFactory**() *throws* SecurityException
	void	**checkSetScheduler**() *throws* SecurityException
✳		**RealtimeSecurity**()

RealtimeSystem   javax.realtime

Object
  ➡RealtimeSystem

✍■	byte	**BIG_ENDIAN**
✍■	byte	**BYTE_ORDER**
❏	GarbageCollector	**currentGC**()
	int	**getConcurrentLocksUsed**()
	int	**getMaximumConcurrentLocks**()
❏	RealtimeSecurity	**getSecurityManager**()
✍■	byte	**LITTLE_ENDIAN**
	void	**setMaximumConcurrentLocks**(int number)
	void	**setMaximumConcurrentLocks**(int number, boolean hard)
❏	void	**setSecurityManager**(RealtimeSecurity manager) *throws* SecurityException

RealtimeThread   javax.realtime

Object
  ➡Thread   Runnable
    ➡RealtimeThread   Schedulable

	void	**addToFeasibility**()
❏	RealtimeThread	**currentRealtimeThread**()
	void	**deschedulePeriodic**()

	MemoryArea	**getMemoryArea**()
	MemoryParameters	**getMemoryParameters**()
	ProcessingGroupParam- eters	**getProcessingGroupParameters**()
	ReleaseParameters	**getReleaseParameters**()
	Scheduler	**getScheduler**()
	SchedulingParameters	**getSchedulingParameters**()
	void	**interrupt**()
❊		**RealtimeThread**()
❊		**RealtimeThread**(SchedulingParameters scheduling)
❊		**RealtimeThread**(SchedulingParameters scheduling, ReleaseParameters release)
❊		**RealtimeThread**(SchedulingParameters scheduling, ReleaseParameters release, MemoryParameters memory, MemoryArea area, ProcessingGroupParameters group, Runnable logic)
	void	**removeFromFeasibility**()
	void	**schedulePeriodic**()
	void	**setMemoryParameters**(MemoryParameters parameters)
	void	**setProcessingGroupParameters**(ProcessingGroupPara- meters parameters)
	void	**setReleaseParameters**(ReleaseParameters parameters)
	void	**setScheduler**(Scheduler scheduler) *throws* IllegalThreadStateException
	void	**setSchedulingParameters**(SchedulingParameters sched- uling)
❑	void	**sleep**(Clock clock, HighResolutionTime time) *throws* InterruptedException
❑	void	**sleep**(HighResolutionTime time) *throws* InterruptedException
	boolean	**waitForNextPeriod**() *throws* IllegalThreadStateException

RelativeTime   javax.realtime

```
Object
   ➡HighResolutionTime                    Comparable
      ➡RelativeTime
```

	AbsoluteTime	**absolute**(Clock clock, AbsoluteTime destination)
	RelativeTime	**add**(long millis, int nanos)
	RelativeTime	**add**(long millis, int nanos, RelativeTime destination)
●	RelativeTime	**add**(RelativeTime time)
	RelativeTime	**add**(RelativeTime time, RelativeTime destination)
	void	**addInterarrivalTo**(AbsoluteTime destination)
	RelativeTime	**getInterarrivalTime**(RelativeTime destination)
❊		**RelativeTime**()
❊		**RelativeTime**(long millis, int nanos)
❊		**RelativeTime**(RelativeTime time)

●	RelativeTime **subtract**(RelativeTime time)
	RelativeTime **subtract**(RelativeTime time, RelativeTime destination)
	String **toString**()

ReleaseParameters   `javax.realtime`

Object
   ➡ReleaseParameters

	RelativeTime **getCost**()
	AsyncEventHandler **getCostOverrunHandler**()
	RelativeTime **getDeadline**()
	AsyncEventHandler **getDeadlineMissHandler**()
✲◆	**ReleaseParameters**(RelativeTime cost, RelativeTime deadline, AsyncEventHandler overrunHandler, AsyncEventHandler missHandler)
	void **setCost**(RelativeTime cost)
	void **setCostOverrunHandler**(AsyncEventHandler handler)
	void **setDeadline**(RelativeTime deadline)
	void **setDeadlineMissHandler**(AsyncEventHandler handler)

ResourceLimitError   `javax.realtime`

Object
   ➡Throwable   java.io.Serializable
      ➡Error
         ➡ResourceLimitError

✲	**ResourceLimitError**()
✲	**ResourceLimitError**(String description)

Schedulable   `javax.realtime`

Schedulable   Runnable

	void **addToFeasibility**()
	MemoryParameters **getMemoryParameters**()
	ReleaseParameters **getReleaseParameters**()
	Scheduler **getScheduler**()
	SchedulingParameters **getSchedulingParameters**()
	void **removeFromFeasibility**()
	void **setMemoryParameters**(MemoryParameters memory)
	void **setReleaseParameters**(ReleaseParameters release)
	void **setScheduler**(Scheduler scheduler)
	void **setSchedulingParameters**(SchedulingParameters scheduling)

Scheduler `javax.realtime`

```
Object
  ➥Scheduler
```

○◆	void	**addToFeasibility**(Schedulable schedulable)
	boolean	**changeIfFeasible**(Schedulable schedulable, ReleaseParameters release, MemoryParameters memory)
❑	Scheduler	**getDefaultScheduler**()
○	String	**getPolicyName**()
○	boolean	**isFeasible**()
○◆	void	**removeFromFeasibility**(Schedulable schedulable)
✳		**Scheduler**()
❑	void	**setDefaultScheduler**(Scheduler scheduler)

SchedulingParameters `javax.realtime`

```
Object
  ➥SchedulingParameters
```

✳		**SchedulingParameters**()

ScopedMemory `javax.realtime`

```
Object
  ➥MemoryArea
    ➥ScopedMemory
```

	void	**enter**(Runnable logic)
	int	**getMaximumSize**()
	MemoryArea	**getOuterScope**()
	Object	**getPortal**()
✳		**ScopedMemory**(long size)
	void	**setPortal**(Object object)

ScopedPhysicalMemory   `javax.realtime`

Object
→ MemoryArea
    → ScopedMemory
        → ScopedPhysicalMemory

❏	ScopedPhysicalMemory **create**(Object type, long base, long size) *throws* SecurityException, SizeOutOfBoundsException, OffsetOutOfBoundsException, UnsupportedPhysicalMemoryException
✳◆	**ScopedPhysicalMemory**(long base, long size)
✳◆	**ScopedPhysicalMemory**(ScopedPhysicalMemory memory, long base, long size)
❏	void **setFactory**(PhysicalMemoryFactory factory)

SizeOutOfBoundsException   `javax.realtime`

Object
→ Throwable   java.io.Serializable
    → Exception
        → SizeOutOfBoundsException

✳	**SizeOutOfBoundsException**()
✳	**SizeOutOfBoundsException**(String description)

SporadicParameters   `javax.realtime`

Object
→ ReleaseParameters
    → AperiodicParameters
        → SporadicParameters

	RelativeTime **getMinimumInterarrival**()
	void **setMinimumInterarrival**(RelativeTime minimum)
✳	**SporadicParameters**(RelativeTime minInterarrival, RelativeTime cost, RelativeTime deadline, AsyncEventHandler overrunHandler, AsyncEventHandler missHandler)

ThrowBoundaryError   `javax.realtime`

Object
→ Throwable   java.io.Serializable
    → Error
        → ThrowBoundaryError

✳	**ThrowBoundaryError**()
✳	**ThrowBoundaryError**(String description)

Timed   javax.realtime

```
Object
  ➡Throwable                              java.io.Serializable
     ➡Exception
        ➡InterruptedException
           ➡AsynchronouslyInterruptedException
              ➡Timed
```

	boolean **doInterruptible**(Interruptible logic)
	void **resetTime**(HighResolutionTime time)
✳	**Timed**(HighResolutionTime time) *throws* IllegalArgumentException

Timer   javax.realtime

```
Object
  ➡AsyncEvent
     ➡Timer
```

	ReleaseParameters **createReleaseParameters**()
	void **disable**()
	void **enable**()
	Clock **getClock**()
	AbsoluteTime **getFireTime**()
	void **reschedule**(HighResolutionTime time)
	void **start**()
✳◆	**Timer**(HighResolutionTime t, Clockc, AsyncEventHandler handler)

UnsupportedPhysicalMemo-ryException   javax.realtime

```
Object
  ➡Throwable                              java.io.Serializable
     ➡Exception
        ➡UnsupportedPhysicalMemoryException
```

✳	**UnsupportedPhysicalMemoryException**()
✳	**UnsupportedPhysicalMemoryException**(String description)

VTMemory   javax.realtime

```
Object
  ➥MemoryArea
      ➥ScopedMemory
          ➥VTMemory
```

✳	**VTMemory**(int initial, int maximum)

WaitFreeDequeue   javax.realtime

```
Object
  ➥WaitFreeDequeue
```

Object	**blockingRead**()
boolean	**blockingWrite**(Object object) *throws* MemoryScopeException
boolean	**force**(Object object)
Object	**nonBlockingRead**()
boolean	**nonBlockingWrite**(Object object) *throws* MemoryScopeException
✳	**WaitFreeDequeue**(Thread writer, Thread reader, int maximum, MemoryArea area) *throws* IllegalArgumentException, IllegalAccessException, ClassNotFoundException, InstantiationException

WaitFreeReadQueue   javax.realtime

```
Object
  ➥WaitFreeReadQueue
```

void	**clear**()
boolean	**isEmpty**()
boolean	**isFull**()
Object	**read**()
int	**size**()
void	**waitForData**()
✳	**WaitFreeReadQueue**(Thread writer, Thread reader, int maximum, MemoryArea memory) *throws* IllegalArgumentException, InstantiationException, ClassNotFoundException, IllegalAccessException
✳	**WaitFreeReadQueue**(Thread writer, Thread reader, int maximum, MemoryArea memory, boolean notify) *throws* IllegalArgumentException, InstantiationException, ClassNotFoundException, IllegalAccessException
boolean	**write**(Object object) *throws* MemoryScopeException

WaitFreeWriteQueue   javax.realtime

```
Object
    ➥WaitFreeWriteQueue
```

void	**bind**(Thread writer, Thread reader, MemoryArea memory) *throws* IllegalArgumentException, IllegalAccessException, InstantiationException
void	**clear**()
boolean	**force**(Object object)
boolean	**isEmpty**()
boolean	**isFull**()
Object	**read**()
int	**size**()
✻	**WaitFreeWriteQueue**(Thread writer, Thread reader, int maximum, MemoryArea memory) *throws* IllegalArgumentException, IllegalAccessException, ClassNotFoundException, InstantiationException
boolean	**write**(Object object) *throws* MemoryScopeException

Bibliography

1. J.H. Anderson, S. Ramamurthy, and K. Jeffay, *Real-Time Computing with Lock-Free Shared Objects*, IEEE Real-Time Systems Symposium 1995, pp. 28-37.

2. J. Anderson, R. Jain, S. Ramamurthy, *Wait-Free Object-Sharing Schemes for Real-Time Uniprocessors and Multiprocessors*, IEEE Real-Time Systems Symposium 1997, pp. 111-122.

3. H. Attiya and N.A. Lynch, *Time Bounds for Real-Time Process Control in the Presence of Timing Uncertainty*, IEEE Real-Time Systems Symposium 1989, pp. 268-284.

4. T.P. Baker and A. Shaw, *The Cyclic Executive Model and Ada*, IEEE Real-Time Systems Symposium 1988, pp. 120-129.

5. T.P. Baker, *A Stack-Based Resource Allocation Policy for Realtime Processes*, IEEE Real-Time Systems Symposium 1990, pp. 191-200.

6. T. Baker and O. Pazy, *Real-Time Features for Ada 9X*, IEEE Real-Time Systems Symposium 1991, pp. 172-180.

7. S.K. Baruah, A.K. Mok, and L.E. Rosier, *Preemptively Scheduling Hard-Real-Time Sporadic Tasks on One Processor*, IEEE Real-Time Systems Symposium 1990, pp. 182-190.

8. L. Carnahan and M. Ruark (eds.), *Requirements for Real-Time Extensions for the Java Platform*, National Institute of Standards and Technology, September 1999. Available at http://www.nist.gov/rt-java.

9. P. Chan, R. Lee, and D. Kramer, *The Java Class Libraries, Second Edition, Volume 1, Supplement for the Java 2 Platform, Standard Edition, v1.2,* Addison-Wesley, 1999.

10. M.-Z. Chen and K.J. Lin, *A Priority Ceiling Protocol for Multiple-Instance Resources*, IEEE Real-Time Systems Symposium 1991, pp. 140-149.

11. S. Cheng, J.A. Stankovic, and K. Ramamritham, *Dynamic Scheduling of Groups of Tasks with Precedence Constraints in Distributed Hard Real-Time Systems*, IEEE Real-Time Systems Symposium 1986, pp. 166-174.

12. R.I. Davis, K. W. Tindell, and A. Burns, *Scheduling Slack Time in Fixed Priority Preemptive Systems*, IEEE Real-Time Systems Symposium 1993, pp. 222-231.

13. B.O. Gallmeister and C. Lanier, *Early Experience with POSIX 1003.4 and POSIX 1003.4a*, IEEE Real-Time Systems Symposium 1991, pp. 190-198.

14. J. Gosling, B. Joy, and G. Steele, *The Java Language Specification*, Addison-Wesley, 1996.

15. M.L. Green, E.Y.S. Lee, S. Majumdar, D.C. Shannon, *A Distributed Real Time Operating System*, IEEE Real-Time Systems Symposium 1980, pp. 175-184.

16. M.G. Harbour, M.H. Klein, and J.P. Lehoczky, *Fixed Priority Scheduling of Periodic Tasks with Varying Execution Priority*, IEEE Real-Time Systems Symposium 1991, pp. 116-128.

17. F. Jahanian and A.K. Mok, *A Graph-Theoretic Approach for Timing Analysis in Real Time Logic*, IEEE Real-Time Systems Symposium 1986, pp. 98-108.

18. K. Jeffay, *Analysis of a Synchronization and Scheduling Discipline for Real-Time Tasks with Preemption Constraints*, IEEE Real-Time Systems Symposium 1989, pp. 295-307.

19. K. Jeffay, D.F. Stanat, and C.U. Martel , *On Non-Preemptive Scheduling of Periodic and SporadicTasks* , IEEE Real-Time Systems Symposium 1991, pp. 129-139.

20. K. Jeffay, *Scheduling Sporadic Tasks with Shared Resources in Hard-Real-Time Systems*, IEEE Real-Time Systems Symposium 1992, pp. 89-99.

21. K. Jeffay and D.L. Stone, *Accounting for Interrupt Handling Costs in Dynamic Priority Task Systems*, IEEE Real-Time Systems Symposium 1993, pp. 212-221.

22. K. Jeffay and D. Bennett, *A Rate-Based Execution Abstraction for Multimedia Computing*, Proceedings of the 5th International Workshop on Network and Operating System Support for Digital Audio and Video (Apr. 1995).

23. E.D. Jensen, C.D. Locke, and H. Tokuda, *A Time-Driven Scheduling Model for Real-Time Operating Systems*, IEEE Real-Time Systems Symposium 1985, pp. 112-133.

24. Mark S. Johnstone, *Non-Compacting Memory Allocation and Real-Time Garbage Collection*, Ph.D. dissertation, The University of Texas at Austin, December 1997.

25. M.B. Jones, *Adaptive Real-Time Resource Management Supporting Modular Composition of Digital Multimedia Services*, Proceedings of the 4th International Workshop on Network and Operating System Support for Digital Audio and Video (Nov. 1993).

26. M.B. Jones, P.J. Leach, R.P. Draves, and J.S. Barrera, *Support for User-centric Modular Real-Time Resource Management in the Rialto Operating System*, Proceedings of the 5th International Workshop on Network and Operating System Support for Digital Audio and Video (Apr. 1995).

27. I. Lee and S.B. Davidson, *Protocols for Timed Synchronous Process Communications*, IEEE Real-Time Systems Symposium 1986, pp. 120-137.

28. J.P. Lehoczky, L. Sha, and J.K. Strosnider, *Enhanced Aperiodic Responsiveness in Hard Real-Time Environments*, IEEE Real-Time Systems Symposium 1987, pp. 261-270.

29. J. Lehoczky, L. Sha, and Y. Ding, *The Rate Monotonic Scheduling Algorithm: Exact Characterization and Average Case Behavior*, IEEE Real-Time Systems Symposium 1989, pp. 166-171.

30. J.P. Lehoczky and T.P. Baker, *Fixed Priority Scheduling of PeriodicTask Sets with Arbitrary Deadlines*, IEEE Real-Time Systems Symposium 1990, pp. 201-213.

31. J.P. Lehoczky and S. Ramos-Thuel, *An Optimal Algorithm for Scheduling Soft-Aperiodic Tasks in Fixed-Priority Preemptive System*, IEEE Real-Time Systems Symposium 1992, pp. 110-124.

32. K.-J. Lin, S. Natarajan, and J.W.-S. Liu, *Imprecise Results: Utilizing Partial Computations in Real-Time Systems*, IEEE Real-Time Systems Symposium 1987, pp. 210-218.

33. T. Lindholm and F. Yellin, *The JavaVirtual Machine Specification, Second Edition,* Addison-Wesley, 1999.

34. C.L. Liu and J.W. Layland, *Scheduling Algorithms for Multiprogramming in a Hard Real-Time Environment*, JACM 20, 1 (Jan. 1973), pp. 46-61.

35. J.W.-S. Liu, K.-J. Lin, and S. Natarajan, *Scheduling Real-Time, Periodic Jobs Using Imprecise Results*, IEEE Real-Time Systems Symposium 1987, pp. 252-260.

36. C. Lizzi, *Enabling Deadline Scheduling for Java Real-Time Computing*, IEEE Real-Time Systems Symposium 1999.

37. C.D. Locke, D.R. Vogel, and T.J. Mesler, *Building a Predictable Avionics Platform in Ada: A Case Study*, IEEE Real-Time Systems Symposium 1991, pp. 180-189.

38. N. Lynch and N. Shavit, *Timing-Based Mutual Exclusion*, IEEE Real-Time Systems Symposium 1992, pp. 2-11.

39. C.W. Mercer and H. Tokuda, *Preemptibility in Real-Time Operating Systems*, IEEE Real-Time Systems Symposium 1992, pp. 78-88.

40. C.W. Mercer, S. Savage, and H. Tokuda, *Processor Capacity Reserves for Multimedia Operating Systems*, Proceedings of the IEEE International Conference on Multimedia Computing and Systems (May 1994).

41. A. Miyoshi, T. Kitayama, H. Tokuda, *Implementation and Evaluation of Real-Time Java Threads*, IEEE Real-Time Systems Symposium 1997, pp. 166-175.

42. J.S. Ostroff and W.M. Wonham, *Modelling, Specifying and Verifying Real-Time Embedded Computer Systems*, IEEE Real-Time Systems Symposium 1987, pp. 124-132.

43. *Portable Operating System Interface (POSIX®) Part 1: System Application Program Interface*, International Standard ISO/IEC 9945-1: 1996 (E) IEEE Std 1003.1, 1996 Edition, The Institute of Electrical and Electronics Engineers, Inc. 1996.

44. R. Rajkumar, L. Sha, and J.P. Lehoczky, *On Countering the Effects of Cycle-Stealing in a Hard Real-Time Environment*, IEEE Real-Time Systems Symposium 1987, pp. 2-11.

45. R. Rajkumar, L. Sha, and J.P. Lehoczky, *Real-Time Synchronization Protocols for Multiprocessors*, IEEE Real-Time Systems Symposium 1988, pp. 259-271.

46. S. Ramos-Thuel and J.P. Lehoczky, *On-Line Scheduling of Hard Deadline Aperiodic Tasks in Fixed-Priority Systems*, IEEE Real-Time Systems Symposium 1993, pp. 160-171.

47. L. Sha, J.P. Lehoczky, and R. Rajkumar, *Solutions for Some Practical Problems in Prioritized Preemptive Scheduling*, IEEE Real-Time Systems Symposium 1986, pp. 181-193.

48. L. Sha, R. Rajkumar, and J. Lehoczky, *Priority Inheritance Protocols: An Approach to Real-Time Synchronization*, IEEE Transactions on Computers, Sept., 1990.

49. L. Sha, R. Rajkumar, and J. Lehoczky, *Real-Time Computing using Futurebus+*, IEEE Micro, June, 1991.

50. A.C. Shaw, *Software Clocks, Concurrent Programming, and Slice-Based Scheduling*, IEEE Real-Time Systems Symposium 1986, pp. 14-19.

51. F. Siebert, *Real-Time Garbage Collection in Multi-Threaded Systems on a Single Processor*, IEEE Real-Time Systems Symposium 1999.

52. B. Sprunt, J. Lehoczky, and L. Sha, *Exploiting Unused Periodic Time for Aperiodic Service Using the Extended Priority Exchange Algorithm*, IEEE Real-Time Systems Symposium 1988, pp. 251-258.

53. Sun Microsystems, Inc., *The Java Community Process Manual*, December 1998, Available at http://java.sun.com/aboutJava/communityprocess/ java_community_process.html.

54. S.R. Thuel and J.P. Lehoczky, *Algorithms for Scheduling Hard Aperiodic Tasks in Fixed-Priority Systems Using Slack Stealing*, IEEE Real-Time Systems Symposium 1994, pp. 22-35.

55. H. Tokuda, J.W. Wendorf, and H.-Y. Wang, *Implementation of a Time-Driven Scheduler for Real-Time Operating System*, IEEE Real-Time Systems Symposium 1987, pp. 271-280.

56. D.M. Washabaugh and D. Kafura, *Incremental Garbage Collection of Concurrent Objects for Real-Time Applications*, IEEE Real-Time Systems Symposium 1990, pp. 21-31.

57. P.R. Wilson, M.S. Johnstone, M. Neely, and D. Boles, *Dynamic Storage Allocation: A Survey and Critical Review*, In International Workshop on Memory Management, Kinross, Scotland, UK, September 1995.

58. W. Zhao and K. Ramamritham, *A Virtual Time CSMA Protocol for Hard Real Time Communication*, IEEE Real-Time Systems Symposium 1986, pp. 120-127.

59. W. Zhao and J.A. Stankovic, *Performance Analysis of FCFS and Improved FCFS Scheduling Algorithms for Dynamic Real-Time Computer Systems*, IEEE Real-Time Systems Symposium 1989, pp. 156-165.

Colophon

This specification document was generated from a set of Java and HTML source files. They were compiled using `javadoc` and the doclet-from-hell: `mifdoclet`. The recent development of `mifdoclet` was driven largely by the Real Time for Java Expert Group. We wanted to be able to produce a specification document that had been checked, as much as possible, by whatever compilation tools we could find. The specification source compiles as a Java program, and even contains a scaffold implementation which was used to compile and run the examples.

The `mifdoclet` generates its output in MIF format, which was processed through Adobe FrameMaker, http://www.adobe.com/products/framemaker, a truely wonderful publishing package without which this book would have been much more difficult.

The source files used to produce this specification will eventually be available at http://www.rtj.org.

Index

H

I

T

U

V

W

The Java™ Series

 ISBN 0-201-70433-1

 ISBN 0-201-70323-8

 ISBN 0-201-70393-9

 ISBN 0-201-48558-3

 ISBN 0-201-43299-4

ISBN 0-201-43297-8

 ISBN 0-201-31002-3

 ISBN 0-201-31003-1

 ISBN 0-201-48552-4

 ISBN 0-201-70329-7

 ISBN 0-201-31000-7

 ISBN 0-201-31008-2

 ISBN 0-201-63453-8

 ISBN 0-201-63459-7

 ISBN 0-201-63456-2

 ISBN 0-201-70277-0

 ISBN 0-201-31009-0

 ISBN 0-201-70502-8

 ISBN 0-201-32577-2

 ISBN 0-201-43294-3

 ISBN 0-201-70456-0

 ISBN 0-201-71041-2

 ISBN 0-201-43321-4

 ISBN 0-201-43328-1

 ISBN 0-201-70969-4

Please see our web site (http://www.awl.com/cseng/javaseries)
for more information on these titles.